GUARDIANS
OF THE
COMMUNITY

UNITING COMMUNITIES

THROUGH SIR ROBERT PEEL'S

TIME-HONORED PRINCIPLES

BILLY GROGAN

For more information, contact: billyjgrogan@gmail.com
http://www.topcopleadership.com

Book Cover Design and Interior Formatting by 100Covers.

ISBN - Paperback: 979-8-9905444-0-6
ISBN - Hardcover: 979-8-9905444-1-3
ISBN - Ebook: 979-8-9905444-2-0
ISBN - Audio: 979-8-9905444-3-7

Published by Peel Enterprises, LLC

First Edition: August 2024

Praise for
Guardians of the
Community

Chief Billy Grogan's exploration of principles attributed to Sir Robert Peel serves as a testament to their enduring significance in contemporary policing. With 50 years of experience in law enforcement and 32 of those years as a police chief, I have witnessed firsthand the paramount importance of these foundational principles.

Chief Grogan's presentation, enhanced by compelling examples and insightful case studies, illuminates their indispensable value to both the individual officers on the front lines and the strategic visionaries leading law enforcement agencies. His prose is accessible and inspiring, fostering a renewed appreciation for the timeless wisdom embedded in Peel's principles and reaffirming their pivotal role in shaping ethical, effective, and community-oriented policing.

This book is a must-read for anyone invested in the evolving landscape of law enforcement, offering a harmonious blend of historical perspective and practical application destined to resonate with seasoned officers and the newer generation of police personnel.

Chief Lou Dekmar (Ret)
Past President IACP 2017-2018

In "Guardians of the Community," Chief Billy Grogan delves into the intricate tapestry of policing, tracing its evolution from the historical streets of London to the present-day challenges faced in the United States.

This riveting exploration sheds light on the ever-changing landscape of police recruitment, retention, transparency, crime, and the pivotal role of community relations. Chief Grogan, a seasoned veteran in law enforcement, imparts his extensive knowledge and firsthand experiences, offering invaluable insights into public safety.

This book is not just a resource but an essential read for anyone invested in the safety and well-being of their community, be it public safety professionals or engaged citizens. Join Chief Grogan on this enlightening journey through the heart of community guardianship.

Dr. Cedric Alexander
NBC/MSNBC Senior Law Enforcement Analyst
Public Safety Executive
Past President NOBLE 2014-2015

As a longtime social justice advocate deeply committed to fostering positive relationships between law enforcement and the communities they serve, I commend Chief Billy Grogan for his insightful contribution to this critical dialogue.

In Guardians of the Community, Chief Grogan masterfully explores Sir Robert Peel's timeless principles of policing, offering invaluable insights into how these principles can unite police departments and communities, particularly in challenging times. Drawing from his wealth of experience as a retired law enforcement executive, Chief Grogan provides practical wisdom and real-world examples illuminating the path toward building trust, cooperation, and accountability within law enforcement.

This book is a key read for anyone invested in promoting justice, equity, and unity in our society.

Reverend Markel Hutchins
CEO, Movement Forward, Inc.
Founder, National Faith & Blue Weekend
Board Member, National Law Enforcement Memorial Fund

This book is dedicated to the men and women in law enforcement. With unwavering commitment, you have devoted your lives to the service of others, embodying the essence of sacrifice and community guardianship. Your relentless courage and compassion in the line of duty do not go unseen. I recognize the weight of your pledge to protect and serve, and with profound gratitude, I honor you—the true Guardians of the Community.

CONTENTS

INTRODUCTION

Law enforcement is the cornerstone of a safe and prosperous society, bearing the critical responsibility of maintaining public order and safeguarding the safety and well-being of its citizens. Throughout history, the concept of policing has evolved markedly, adapting to meet the shifting needs and complexities of communities across the globe. Yet, at the core of modern policing are principles established by the visionary statesman Sir Robert Peel.

This book investigates precisely how adherence to Peel's Nine Principles of Policing can forge unity between the police and the community during thriving and tumultuous times.

In the early 19th century, Sir Robert Peel, a notable British politician, and founder of the Metropolitan Police of London, set forth nine fundamental principles that established the groundwork for professional policing. These principles, revolutionary at the time, remain profoundly relevant in today's law enforcement practices.

Widely regarded as the father of modern policing, Peel served as the Prime Minister of the United Kingdom twice in the 19th century. His tenure was marked by several significant reforms that have shaped contemporary British society.

The founding of the London Metropolitan Police Department in 1829 marked a pivotal moment in the history of English law enforcement. The establishment of the Met introduced a professional and centralized system to maintain public order, revolutionizing the concept of policing.

Before the Met's creation, law enforcement in London was disorganized, ineffectual, and marred by corruption. The system depended on unpaid volunteer constables and a few inadequately equipped watchmen to address the growing urban crime in an expanding city. The rise in crime rates, political turmoil, and public discontent necessitated a sweeping overhaul of the policing system. Moreover, the absence of established guidelines or principles led to inconsistent and often arbitrary law enforcement.

On September 29, 1829, Sir Charles Rowan and Richard Mayne inaugurated the London Metropolitan Police with an initial deployment of 1,000 constables. The headquarters at Scotland Yard became the central hub for the new force, grounded in Peel's Nine Principles of Policing. These principles underscored the necessity of crime prevention, the value of public cooperation, and the imperative of police impartiality.

A central innovation of the Met was its organizational structure. London was segmented into police districts supervised by a superintendent responsible for law and order in their area. This centralization fostered better coordination, enhanced communication, and a more efficient response to criminal activity.

Moreover, the Met set new professional standards and practices that elevated the quality of policing in England. Officers were now mandated to wear uniforms, bear identification, and participate in extensive training. This move towards heightened professionalism and discipline played a significant role in regaining the public's trust in the police force.

The London Metropolitan Police adopted a proactive approach to crime prevention. Creating specialized units, such as the Detective Department in 1842, was instrumental in combatting organized crime and investigating complex cases. Implementing regular patrols and introducing new technologies, such as gas lighting and police telegraphs, enhanced the visibility and response time of the force.

Additionally, the Met recognized the importance of maintaining positive relations with the public. Introducing the "*Bobby*" or the "*Peeler*" as a friendly and approachable figure in the community fostered a sense of trust and cooperation. Police officers were encouraged to engage with the public to gather intelligence and build relationships with residents.

The modernization efforts of the London Metropolitan Police profoundly influenced policing across England. Other cities followed London's lead and established police forces, adopting many of the Met's organizational structures and practices. The Metropolitan Police Act of 1839 expanded the Met's jurisdiction beyond city limits, extending its influence throughout London.

The Met's centralized control model, professionalism, and community-oriented policing became the foundation for modern law enforcement agencies worldwide. Its legacy is evident in the principles and practices still upheld by police forces today, emphasizing the significance of public trust, crime prevention, and community engagement.

This book explores Sir Robert Peel's Nine Principles of Policing and examines their enduring relevance and significance in the modern world. It provides a historical context for Peel's principles, offering a deep understanding of the societal challenges during that era and the visionary thinking that led to their development.

Peel's Nine Principles are a timeless guide for effective and responsible policing. They transcend the boundaries of time and geography, offering valuable insights into the core values that underpin law enforcement and their application to the complex issues faced by today's police forces.

By fully comprehending and adhering to these principles, police agencies are better equipped to address the complexities of our rapidly changing society while maintaining the highest standards of professionalism, public trust, and safeguarding individual rights.

In the following chapters, this book will examine each of Sir Robert Peel's Nine Principles in-depth, dissecting their intended purpose and underscoring their lasting significance in modern law enforcement. We begin with Principle #1, which defines the police's core mission: to protect life and property, prevent and detect crime, and preserve public peace.

We will then consider Principle #2, highlighting the necessity for public approval and support. This section will discuss the imperative of nurturing positive community relations and the crucial role community policing plays in building cooperation and trust.

As we progress chapter by chapter, the book will dissect the profound influence each principle has had on developing policing strategies and tactics. We will examine the delicate balance between public safety and individual freedoms, the concept of policing by consent rather than force, and the premise that physical force should be a measure of last resort.

Moreover, the discussion will extend to the principles that advocate for police neutrality and impartiality, the importance of accountability and transparency, and the essential need for a competent and professional police service. Through case studies and real-world scenarios, we will bring to life each principle's practical implementation and current pertinence.

Advancing through the narrative, we will confront the challenges law enforcement agencies face and assess how Peel's principles can direct and shape effective strategies in response to these trials. From the intricacies of cybercrime and the threats of terrorism to the dynamics of community relations and the integration of emerging technologies, we will unravel the complex issues confronting police forces today.

In the United States' formative years, the nation adopted England's common law justice system. This system was upheld by various law enforcement figures, including sheriffs, watchmen, constables, and vigilantes, who were tasked with ensuring the safety and security of citizens. During this period, crime was primarily local, characterized by thefts, disputes, and assaults with known acquaintances.

As urban areas expanded, the necessity for a dedicated, full-time municipal police force became apparent. The New York Police Department, established in 1845, was the first in the United States. The formation of the New Orleans Police Department, the Cincinnati Police Department, the Boston Police Department, and the Philadephia Police Department soon followed.[1]

The formation of police departments introduced significant reforms in law enforcement. These institutions standardized uniforms, training, and procedures. Cities transitioned from relying on volunteers to employing dedicated officers focused on maintaining public order and preventing crime.

This shift from a reactive to a proactive stance in law enforcement represented a pivotal development in American policing. Inspired by the London Metropolitan Police, these early departments adopted a quasi-military command structure.

Initially, police forces served as extensions of the political landscape, controlled by local politicians who influenced wards and neighborhoods. However, as the departments matured, they moved towards greater professionalism.

Today, crime has also changed, presenting unprecedented challenges. It extends from the tangible streets to the digital realm and expands from local neighborhoods to a global stage. The landscape of crime is more intricate and demanding than ever.

The original recruitment of officers was marred by patronage over merit, leading to inefficiency, discrimination, and corruption. This has

---

[1] "Early Police in the United States," Encyclopedia Britannica, accessed June 3, 2023, https://www.britannica.com/topic/police/Early-police-in-the-United-States.

drastically changed with the introduction of civil service systems, resulting in a better-trained and educated police force.

Consequently, policing became a sought-after and esteemed profession. Many police departments experienced an influx of candidates, allowing them to select from a vast pool of applicants and maintain hiring waitlists. Of course, a lot has changed recruitment-wise in recent years. More on that topic later.

Law enforcement has undergone substantial changes, especially in the realm of professionalization. This evolution has seen the establishment of uniform practices, heightened educational prerequisites, advanced training, and an emphasis on ethical behavior. The field's professionalization has been instrumental in increasing the value and credibility of police agencies, building community trust, and contributing to the safety of society.

Comprehensive training programs are the backbone of professionalizing law enforcement. Agencies now acknowledge the importance of ongoing education to keep pace with the latest technologies, legal requirements, and community policing strategies.

Training curricula now cover many subjects, such as cultural diversity, implicit bias, crisis intervention, forensic science, and conflict resolution. Practical exercises and scenario-based training are integral in creating realistic settings to prepare officers for effective decision-making in high-pressure situations.

In recent years, there has been a discernible shift in the profile of those seeking careers in law enforcement. Historically, a significant portion of the police force comprised ex-military personnel who brought a *'live to work'* mentality to the job. These individuals often adapted well to the quasi-military structure of police departments, reflecting their previous service. Today, however, there is an increasing trend of officers who prioritize work-life balance, embodying a *'work to live'* philosophy.[2]

Law enforcement agencies globally are undergoing a transformation as officers from the baby boomer and Generation X approach retirement.

---

[2] "A Crisis Facing Law Enforcement Recruiting in the 21st Century," Police Chief Magazine, accessed June 3, 2023, https://www.policechiefmagazine. org/a-crisis-facing-law-enforcement-recruiting-in-the-21st-century/.

This demographic shift is reshaping the policing landscape, presenting new challenges and opportunities for the incoming workforce.

Several factors are accelerating the retirement of baby boomers and Generation X from law enforcement roles. Attractive retirement benefits and pension plans entice older officers to leave the force. Furthermore, the physically demanding nature of police work can pose increasing challenges as officers age. Additionally, shifts in the social and political climate, along with intensified scrutiny of police conduct, have contributed to a sense of frustration among veteran officers.

The retirement of these seasoned officers results in a significant loss of accumulated knowledge and practical expertise that is difficult to replace. Their departure can affect critical areas such as decision-making, problem-solving, and mentoring recruits.

However, this generational turnover also opens doors for integrating modern policing techniques and philosophies. Younger generations entering the force are introducing innovative perspectives, varied experiences, and a tech-savvy approach to their duties. This transition is conducive to advancing community-focused policing, analytical decision-making, and a stronger focus on conflict de-escalation and community involvement.

The wave of retirements and a decrease in new applicants have precipitated a recruitment and retention crisis for many law enforcement agencies. According to a 2023 survey of police recruitment and retention completed by the Police Executive Research Forum (PERF), there were 50 % more resignations in 2022 compared to 2019, and retirements increased by 20 % in the agencies responding to the survey.[3] These numbers are not sustainable in the long run.

Contributing to this issue are the diminishing public trust and support for law enforcement, influenced by high-profile instances of police misconduct, allegations of racial bias, and controversial uses of force.

Moreover, negative portrayals of police in the media and on social media platforms have amplified movements like *"defund the police"* and fostered hostility towards law enforcement, creating an environment that can be unwelcoming and even hostile for officers.

---

[3] Police Executive Research Forum (PERF), "2023 Survey on Police Staffing," accessed May 31, 2023, https://www.policeforum.org/staffing2023.

While Sir Robert Peel is traditionally recognized for establishing the Nine Principles of Policing, recent research indicates that Charles Rowan and Richard Mayne, the inaugural Joint Commissioners of the MET, may have been the actual architects of these principles. Since these principles are a staple of law enforcement training, acknowledging the possibility of their true origins is crucial.

Before Sir Robert Peel's influence, pivotal figures such as Patrick Colquhoun and Jeremy Bentham were instrumental in shaping the foundational concepts of modern policing. Colquhoun, a Scottish magistrate, was an early proponent of the preventative role of the police, advocating for strategic collaboration between the police force and the community and implementing preventive patrols.

Jeremy Bentham, an English philosopher, promoted a systematic and analytical approach to law enforcement. He emphasized deterrence and the *'principle of utility,'* which suggests that the best policy or action maximizes overall happiness and reduces suffering.[4]

While Sir Robert Peel may not have been the sole architect of the Nine Principles of Policing, his name became synonymous with them due to his significant reforms and the establishment of the MET. The principles advocate for crime prevention, the cultivation of public trust, and the impartial enforcement of laws. They further highlight the importance of police accountability, the judicious use of force, and the imperative for independence from political influence.

The debate over their authorship does not diminish their foundational importance. When these principles were first applied in 1829, they were revolutionary, marking a dramatic departure from the law enforcement norms of the time.

Their enduring relevance is a testament to their foundational nature, as they continue to guide modern policing with their forward-thinking approach to maintaining public order and ensuring justice.

Charles Reith, in his analysis of policing history, stated,

"It was a philosophy of policing unique in history and throughout the world because it derived not from fear but almost exclusively from public cooperation

---

[4] "Policing the Poor: A Brief Introduction to Patrick Colquhoun," J. M. Moore, accessed June 3, 2023, https://jmmoore.org/2022/09/08/policing-the-poor-a-brief-introduction-to-patrick-colquhoun/.

with the police, induced by them designedly by behavior which secures and maintains for them the approval, respect, and affection of the public."[5]

The resonance of Peel's principles with today's societal needs is striking. Indeed, these principles of policing are as relevant now as ever. They stand as pillars for law enforcement agencies worldwide, offering a robust framework to uphold public order, protect individual liberties, and cultivate trust between the police and the communities they serve.

By comprehending their historical significance and acknowledging their timeless pertinence, we can forge a path toward a more secure and united society for the twenty-first century and beyond.

Each chapter of this book culminates in a series of reflective questions and proposed actions to bridge the gap between local police officers and the citizens they serve. These questions invite officers to contemplate and critically assess their department's alignment with Peel's principles. For citizens, the questions offer insights and encourage a deeper understanding of—and, if necessary, a dialogue about—the standards by which their police department operates.

---

[5] "Definition of Policing by Consent," GOV.UK, accessed June 3, 2023, https://www.gov.uk/government/publications/policing-by-consent/definition-of-policing-by-consent.

PRINCIPLE #1

*To **prevent** crime and disorder, as an **alternative** to their repression by military force and **severity** of legal punishment.*

Originally conceived nearly two centuries ago, this principle remains profoundly significant today. Given the ever-evolving dynamics of crime and society, its relevance is perhaps even greater now.

Preventing crime is a fundamental duty of law enforcement, yet many leaders in the field have become preoccupied with other pressing concerns of the modern age. The emphasis has shifted to officer recruitment and retention, technological advancements, social media presence, liability issues, the use of force, and managing the public's perception of the police, among other critical issues.

While these matters certainly warrant attention, we must maintain sight of our foundational obligation to prevent crime and maintain order.

Sir Robert Peel cautioned against over-reliance on aggressive enforcement tactics, which he described as *"repression by military force."* In today's terms, this means an overemphasis on specialized units executing high-intensity enforcement actions as the sole strategy for combating crime. This approach alone is insufficient.

At its heart, this Peelian principle champions proactive policing. It underscores that the police's role is not merely to respond to crimes but to prevent them from occurring. Police officers must be proactive, utilizing diverse strategies and tactics to anticipate and prevent criminal activities.

One of the most critical contemporary applications of this principle is community policing. This strategy fosters collaboration between police officers and community members, enabling them to identify and solve issues jointly. Building strong community relationships allows officers to gain deeper insights into residents' unique challenges. Together, they can devise effective measures to curb crime and disorder.

Adopting a community policing philosophy can yield numerous benefits for law enforcement agencies. These benefits include heightened officer morale and increased retention rates as officers feel more engaged and supported. This approach also enhances the potential for attracting quality recruits. Furthermore, community policing can strengthen trust and relations between the agency and the public, fostering a cooperative environment. Safety for both officers and citizens can see notable improvements, and overall, the department may experience gains in efficiency due to the supportive network fostered by community collaboration.[6]

Educating the community plays a critical role in crime prevention as well. Initiatives like Lock, Take, Hide, Neighborhood Watch, Citizen Police Academy, the R.A.D. System of Self-Defense and similar programs are essential in empowering citizens. They transform community members into proactive partners in law enforcement's efforts to deter crime.

The impact of crime prevention programs cannot be overstated—they can be the turning point in maintaining community safety.

Law enforcement leaders must prioritize reducing crime and disorder. Addressing such complex issues requires open dialogue, so it's vital to dedicate time during staff meetings, strategic planning sessions, roll calls, and other gatherings to discussing and formulating strategies for crime prevention.

The adage *"out of sight, out of mind"* aptly applies here—without conversation, there is no action. Thus, acknowledging, and incentivizing individuals who develop effective crime prevention initiatives is crucial.

---

[6]   "The Top Benefits of Community Policing," ZenCity Blog, accessed June 3, 2023, https://zencity.io/blog/the-top-benefits-of-community-policing/.

By celebrating these achievements, law enforcement agencies honor these efforts and set a clear standard for the values and behaviors they seek to promote within their ranks.

The task of preventing crime today is undoubtedly challenging, and the complexity of crime has grown exponentially since the days of Sir Robert Peel. However, the fundamental goal of preventing crime remains as critical now as it was back in 1829.

The Routine Activity Theory offers a framework developed by criminologists to analyze how social and environmental factors converge to facilitate criminal acts. Central to this theory are three elements: a potential offender, a suitable target, and the lack of a capable guardian. The convergence of these elements creates a crime opportunity, with each component integral to the potential for a criminal incident.[7] Understanding this theory can significantly enhance law enforcement efforts in crime prevention.

The "*offender*" represents those who commit the crime. By studying their behaviors and patterns, law enforcement can proactively identify potential suspects and tailor their strategies effectively. This can include targeting hotspots, enhancing surveillance, and focusing investigations where they are most needed.

The "*target*" is the person or property at risk of victimization. Analyzing which target offenders choose allows the police to pinpoint vulnerable individuals, locations, or assets. Recognizing these patterns enables the implementation of preventive measures such as community alerts, security upgrades, and increased patrols.

The "*absence of a capable guardian*" indicates a lack of protective measures or presence to deter crime. Factors might include poor lighting, insufficient security, or a low police presence. Addressing these deficiencies can involve reallocating resources, intensifying community involvement, and fostering crime prevention programs.

By applying the Routine Activity Theory, police departments can anticipate criminal actions and disrupt the crime triangle. This requires thorough analysis and a strategic approach to diminish criminal opportunities.

---

[7]   "Routine Activities Theory: Definition of the Routine Activity Approach to Crime," CriminologyWeb, accessed June 3, 2023, https://criminologyweb.com/routine-activities-theory-definition-of-the-routine-activity-approach-to-crime/.

However, this theory should not be the sole tactic but part of a broader crime prevention strategy. Effective use of this theory involves integrating advanced technology and data analytics to reveal patterns, assess risks, and refine policing methods.

Collaboration with local government, community groups, and businesses is essential to tackle broader crime-contributing factors. This joint effort can strengthen community ties and encourage active participation in crime prevention.

Focusing on prevention rather than solely on reaction can significantly minimize the chances for crime to occur. By altering the environment and targeting potential offenders based on robust data, police can create less crime-prone conditions.

Adept crime analysts can use data to craft comprehensive strategies that focus on problem areas and habitual offenders while bolstering the presence of guardians.

Technology also plays a pivotal role. While some law enforcement leaders may recognize its necessity, not all fully grasp the extent of its potential benefits. Modern police vehicles, for instance, are equipped with various technologies to aid officers in their duties. Cameras, computers, fingerprint scanners, crime-fighting dashboards, and other devices can enhance response efficiency and ensure thorough documentation.

Predictive policing tools, like Geolitica, harness vast data sets and machine learning to pinpoint likely crime locations and individuals. These models enable strategic resource allocation and proactive measures, potentially reducing crime rates and optimizing law enforcement resources.

Predictive models are most effective in departments with access to large data volumes, where they can analyze and predict with greater accuracy. In such environments, predictive policing can transform the approach to crime prevention from reactive to proactive, significantly impacting community safety.

While the promise of predictive policing is considerable, skepticism and criticism remain regarding its application. Detractors, including some individuals and experts, highlight significant concerns surrounding the use of these models. They point to potential privacy infringements, the risk of reinforcing racial biases, and the incidence of false positives as critical issues that need to be addressed.[8]

Considering these concerns and to avoid potential misuse, police departments must establish robust policies for using predictive policing technologies, accompanied by strict oversight mechanisms to curb any abuses.

Facial recognition technology, particularly software developed by companies like Clearview AI, is another effective crime-fighting tool. This software, capable of rapidly identifying individuals from a vast database of uploaded photos, has sparked significant debate regarding its deployment by law enforcement agencies.

Amidst the debate, privacy concerns and the possibility of misuse are significant issues for technologies like Clearview AI's facial recognition software. On the other hand, proponents highlight its utility, pointing out cases where it has assisted law enforcement in solving crimes and enhancing community safety.[9]

The advent of social media and the ubiquity of surveillance cameras have provided law enforcement with abundant visual data for identifying suspects. Facial recognition software capitalizes on this by rapidly analyzing images and comparing them with its vast database, offering valuable leads to investigators.

The most notable advantage of facial recognition technology is its ability to quickly process and match billions of images, which has proven instrumental in solving complex cases, including those involving child exploitation, human trafficking, and terrorism. For example, since the Dunwoody Police Department started using Clearview AI in 2022, they have been able to identify multiple suspects, solving several cases that might have remained unresolved.

Consider the scenario where a suspect's photo, taken during a vehicle break-in, yields no immediate leads. When the image is processed through Clearview AI, it can return a potential match, which, upon further investigation, can lead to a confirmed identity and subsequent arrest.

---

[8]   Brookings Institution, "Data-Driven Policing's Threat to Our Constitutional Rights," accessed May 31, 2023, https://www.brookings.edu/articles/data-driven-policings-threat-to-our-constitutional-rights/.

[9]   "The Role of AI in Modern Policing," a&s Magazines, accessed June 3, 2023, https://www.asmag.com/showpost/33078.aspx.

Facial recognition can also prove crucial in identifying individuals who are hard to trace or when image quality is suboptimal. Moreover, it can help locate missing persons or those in danger, demonstrating its utility in time-sensitive situations.

Despite these benefits, concerns over privacy violations persist. The technology's reliance on extensive photo databases, often sourced without explicit consent, sparks fear about potential abuse. Law enforcement can mitigate these concerns by implementing strict policies governing the use of such software.

Another significant concern is the risk of bias, with evidence suggesting variability in accuracy across different skin tones, which could result in wrongful identifications. Additionally, the chance of false positives necessitates that facial recognition matches be treated as starting points for investigation rather than conclusive evidence.

While facial recognition presents powerful investigative opportunities, its application within law enforcement must be tempered with careful policy, oversight, and an ongoing commitment to justice and privacy.

License plate reader (LPR) cameras have become increasingly vital in modern law enforcement's arsenal against crime. While the concept isn't new, recent advances have made LPR technology, both fixed and mobile, more accessible and cost-effective, significantly enhancing police capabilities in responding to, investigating, and curbing crime.

Previously, automated LPR technology was prohibitively expensive and predominantly mobile, limiting its widespread adoption. However, the landscape shifted with the advent of Flock Safety in Atlanta, Georgia, in 2017. Flock Safety democratized this technology for broader community use by designing cost-effective cameras for fixed deployment.

Installed on poles or buildings, these fixed LPR cameras capture license plates of passing vehicles, relaying the data to a cloud-based system for processing and analysis. This innovation has bolstered public safety in many ways:

1. **Crime Investigation**: Flock Safety's LPR cameras have proven invaluable in tracking suspects. By capturing a suspect vehicle's license plate, law enforcement can swiftly act, leading to heightened arrest rates and a deterrent effect on crime within communities utilizing these systems.

2. **Crime Deterrence**: LPR cameras can act as a deterrent, reducing the likelihood of criminal activity in monitored zones. While challenging to quantify, there is an observable trend where potential criminals avoid areas with active LPR surveillance.

3. **Traffic Management**: These cameras also gather traffic data, assisting city planners and engineers in optimizing traffic flows and addressing safety concerns in congested areas.

4. **Located Wanted People and Vehicles**: The technology plays a critical role in locating missing or wanted persons and recovering stolen vehicles, contributing to the safety and recovery of assets and individuals.

Flock Safety's model is unique in that it extends the reach of LPR technology to private entities, such as residential communities and businesses, at an affordable cost. Law enforcement's access to data from these private cameras can multiply their reach and responsiveness.

Ultimately, law enforcement's application of such technology is restricted only by imagination and ethical considerations. LPR cameras are a testament to how innovation can transform public safety, providing real-time data that can be harnessed to protect and serve communities effectively.

Sir Robert Peel's phrase concerning the '*severity of legal punishment*' suggests that law enforcement cannot rely solely on the threat of harsh punishment to deter crime. This approach is ineffective because the deterrent power of punishment is contingent on the certainty and swiftness of its application. The criminal justice system is often marred by delays and inefficiencies, weakening the connection between crime and consequence and, thus, diminishing the preventive impact of severe punishment.

Furthermore, the assumption underpinning severe punishment is that potential offenders are rational actors who assess the risks before committing a crime. Yet, criminal behavior is frequently the result of non-rational factors like impulse, need, or environmental influences, including poverty, addiction, or mental health issues. In such instances, the threat of harsh penalties may be far less of a deterrent than anticipated.

An overemphasis on punitive measures also strains the prison system, leading to overcrowded facilities and a heavy fiscal toll on the state. This can detract from rehabilitation efforts, which are critical in reducing repeat offending. Investing in rehabilitation and reintegration programs is often more effective in the long run than implementing excessively harsh penalties.

Naturally, violent offenders warrant different treatment. Those who use a firearm to commit a crime or cause harm to someone should serve an appropriate period of incarceration.

To achieve sustainable crime reduction, a holistic approach is necessary—one that not only enforces the law but also addresses the root causes of criminal behavior through social initiatives, education, and support services. This includes tackling poverty, providing access to quality education, creating employment opportunities, and offering robust substance abuse and mental health support.

Although it is important to address the root causes of crime, the enforcement of existing laws cannot be overlooked.

The implementation of Peel's principle must navigate the delicate balance between proactive policing and the preservation of individual rights and civil liberties. Excessive policing risks infringing on personal freedoms and eroding public trust, which is counterproductive to community safety goals and mutual respect between law enforcement and the populace.

In the face of increasingly complex public safety challenges, law enforcement agencies have opted to form specialized police units. If used properly, these units, equipped with targeted training and resources, are critical in bolstering the overall effectiveness of policing strategies.

The expertise these specialized units bring is invaluable. Focusing on specific threats like narcotics, cybercrime, terrorism, or gang-related activities, they bring a depth of knowledge and a set of skills that are finely tuned to address and dismantle intricate criminal operations.

When law enforcement channels its efforts into specialized domains, the benefits are clear: expedited investigations, heightened intelligence accuracy, and a marked improvement in addressing crime's root causes. The strategic allocation of resources these units facilitate can make the difference in turning the tide against sophisticated criminal elements.

Far from creating a divide, specialized units have the potential to bridge gaps with the communities they serve. Through concerted outreach—partnering with local groups, educational institutions, and civic organizations—these units do more than enforce; they educate, engage, and empower. Initiatives on drug education, anti-gang activities, and other community concerns not only foster awareness but also cultivate a trust that transcends traditional police-community dynamics.

These specialized units can draw on community insights by embedding themselves within the community fabric, earning the trust and collaboration necessary for proactive and preventative policing. This integrated approach fortifies community safety and reinforces communal ties, ensuring law enforcement and the public work together to maintain peace and order.

Deploying specialized units within law enforcement has yielded considerable advantages in the targeted approach to specific criminal activities. However, without meticulous oversight and management, these advantages can be overshadowed by grave risks. The tragic case of Tyre Nichols in Memphis, who died following an encounter with officers from the Street Crimes Operations to Restore Peace in Our Neighborhoods (SCORPION) unit, serves as a stark reminder of these potential perils. In response to this tragedy, Chief Davis disbanded the SCORPION unit permanently.[10]

The dissolution of the SCORPION unit underscores the necessity of stringent checks and balances within specialized police teams. It calls attention to the critical need for these units to operate within the accountability and community safety standards framework. The incident with Tyre Nichols highlighted the importance of ensuring that the power and autonomy granted to specialized units are matched by an equivalent level of oversight and transparent governance.

While specialized units are formulated to reduce high crime rates and address serious threats efficiently, their actions must always align with justice and human rights principles. Policing strategies must be continually assessed to ensure they do not compromise the dignity and safety of the community's individuals. The goal should always be to enhance community relations and mutual trust, which is essential to effective law enforcement.

Chief Davis' decision to disband the SCORPION unit was a definitive measure aimed at reinforcing the ethos of policing by consent rather than force. It serves as a cautionary tale and a learning point for law enforcement

---

[10] "Police special units like the one that killed Tyre Nichols are common. Here's why they've drawn criticism," PBS NewsHour, accessed June 3, 2023, https://www.pbs.org/newshour/nation/police-special-units-like-the-one-that-killed-tyre-nichols-are-common-heres-why-theyve-drawn-criticism.

agencies nationwide on the importance of maintaining a balance between proactive policing and the fundamental rights of citizens.

Law enforcement must extract lessons from such incidents and evolve their strategies and oversight mechanisms. This involves fostering a culture of continuous improvement, ethical conduct, and community engagement within specialized units. Through such dedicated efforts, law enforcement can hope to prevent such tragedies in the future and ensure the security and trust of the communities they serve.

Specialized police units, exemplified by the now-disbanded SCORPION unit, carry out their duties often shrouded in a level of secrecy necessitated by their covert operations. While this cloak of invisibility can be crucial to their effectiveness, it also poses a significant challenge to maintaining transparency and accountability. The hidden nature of their work can lead to situations where allegations of misconduct—be it excessive force or racial profiling—remain unaddressed, slowly chipping away at the bedrock of public trust in law enforcement.

A concept known as mission creep can further complicate the role of specialized units. Originally established with a clear mandate, these units can inadvertently expand their reach, stepping beyond their initial responsibility. This gradual shift can threaten civil liberties and lead to units operating with autonomy that may sidestep the checks and balances designed to safeguard the public's rights.

Therefore, it is imperative that law enforcement leadership enforces rigorous oversight of specialized units. They must proactively investigate all misconduct allegations, ensuring that those within the unit are held to the highest standards of conduct. Transparent operations and accountability are not just expected but required to maintain the integrity of these units and the trust of the public they serve.

The key to circumventing the risks associated with specialized units lies in thorough training and education. Officers within these units must possess the knowledge and skills to prevent crime effectively while simultaneously upholding the freedoms and rights of individuals. Training in de-escalation techniques, conflict resolution, and ethical decision-making is essential. Moreover, there must be a consistent and just system of accountability where officers are answerable for their actions and where ethical standards are not just guidelines but mandatory requirements for all.

In essence, while specialized units are a powerful tool in the law enforcement arsenal, their success is predicated on their ability to operate within a framework that respects the law and the community. Leadership in these units must be vigilant and proactive, ensuring their actions align with the principles of justice and the values of the society they are sworn to protect.

The deployment of specialized units to combat crime is significantly more effective when integrated within the broader framework of a community policing philosophy adopted by the agency.

Modern law enforcement agencies worldwide are committed to proactive crime prevention. By embracing strategies like community policing, intelligence-led policing, and the incorporation of advanced technology, these agencies are shifting from a reactive to a preventative paradigm. This shift is not merely tactical but philosophical, representing a fundamental change in how police view their societal role.

By prioritizing the prevention of crime and disorder, police departments aim to create safer neighborhoods and cement a foundation of trust and mutual respect with the communities they serve. This trust is the cornerstone of a collaborative relationship between the public and the police, essential for society's sustained safety and well-being.

This timeless principle articulated by Sir Robert Peel serves as a beacon, guiding law enforcement towards an ideal of service that is as relevant today as it was in the past. It underscores the need for a forward-thinking approach, where the goal is to prevent and solve crime.

Adhering to these principles and fostering unity between the police force and the public will pave the way for a collaborative effort to create a secure and harmonious society.

Peel's Principles in Practice: Questions for Today's Challenges and Opportunities

Police Officers

1. What proactive policing strategies is your department currently employing to anticipate and prevent crime?

2. How is your department fostering relationships with your community to collaboratively solve issues?

3. What role does community policing play in your department, and how can you improve it?

4. How is your department recognizing and incentivizing officers who develop effective crime prevention initiatives?

5. In what ways is your department utilizing technology, like predictive policing tools, to aid in crime prevention?

6. How is your department addressing concerns about the potential for racial bias and privacy infringements in technologies that is deployed, like facial recognition?

7. What measures does your department take to ensure specialized units operate with accountability and do not exceed their mandates?

8. How does your department balance the necessity of specialized police units with maintaining individual rights and civil liberties?

9. What ongoing training and education does your department provide to ensure officers are equipped to prevent crime while upholding ethical standards?

Citizens

1. How does your local police department prioritize crime prevention and maintain order in your community?
2. What efforts are made to engage with the community and establish trust between citizens and the police?
3. Which community policing initiatives does your department support, and how can citizens get involved?
4. How transparent is the department in its use of surveillance and predictive policing technologies?
5. What steps has your police department taken to minimize racial bias and protect privacy when using technology like facial recognition?
6. How does your department ensure that specialized units, such as those dealing with narcotics or cybercrime, operate without infringing on civil liberties?
7. What opportunities are available for community education on crime prevention and safety?
8. How does your police department utilize data and technology like LPR cameras responsibly?
9. What is your department's approach to dealing with non-rational factors contributing to criminal behavior, such as poverty and mental health issues?
10. How does your department maintain a balance between proactive policing and the preservation of individual rights and freedoms?

PRINCIPLE #2

*To recognise always that the **power** of the police to fulfil their functions and duties **depends** on public **approval** of their existence, **actions**, and behavior and on their ability to secure and maintain public **respect**.*

In law enforcement, an agency's authority is anchored in the legal framework established by local, state, or federal legislation, which empowers officers to perform their duties within their jurisdiction. Yet, the foundation of an agency's power extends beyond legal mandates and is deeply rooted in the consent and support of the populace it serves.

Sir Robert Peel profoundly understood this when he stated in 1829 that the capacity to enforce the law stems from public endorsement. This concept remains a cornerstone of democratic policing. Peel's insight underpins the philosophy that if a law enforcement body opposes the community's principles, its legitimate authority, granted by governmental law, may be challenged or withdrawn by the society it aims to protect.

The reciprocal relationship between the police and the public is fundamental. The community's trust and cooperation fortify an agency's ability to maintain order and public safety. Law enforcement agencies, therefore, must align their operations with the community's values and expectations. When agencies and their officers act with integrity, fairness, and respect for all individuals, they reinforce their legitimacy and strengthen the community's trust.

This alignment is not static but dynamic, requiring continual dialogue, transparency, and responsiveness to the community's evolving values. Law enforcement leaders are responsible for ensuring their agencies remain attuned to the community's voice and adapt policies and practices to maintain and enhance the community's trust.

Law enforcement agencies must self-evaluate and actively participate with community stakeholders to uphold this principle. This process not only promotes accountability but also ensures that policing strategies reflect the community's needs and preserve the fundamental rights of every individual. In essence, law enforcement's true power is a product of its commitment to serving the community with a spirit of collaboration and respect for the democratic values that grant it authority.

On June 17, 2010, the dissolution of the Maywood-Cudahy Police Department stood as a stark reminder of the critical importance of integrity and professionalism in law enforcement. After an extensive investigation, the California attorney general's office issued a damning conclusion. The report highlighted the department was rife with issues. Here is an example from a partial text of the report: *"permeated with sexual innuendo, harassment, vulgarity, discourtesy to members of the public as well as among officers, and had a lack of cultural, racial and ethnic sensitivity and respect."* This failure to uphold the expected standards of conduct compromised the department's legitimacy and eroded the community's trust, ultimately leading to its disbandment.[11]

The dissolution serves as a cautionary tale, emphasizing that the power entrusted to law enforcement agencies is contingent upon their adherence to respect, professionalism, and sensitivity toward the community they serve. When a police department strays from these principles, it fails to fulfill its mandate to protect and serve and risks losing its legitimacy and authority.

---

[11]   Los Angeles Times, "Maywood Lays Off All City Employees, Becomes 1st in Nation to Outsource All City Services," June 17, 2010, accessed May 31, 2023, https://www.latimes.com/local/la-xpm-2010-jun-17-la-me-maywood-pd-20100617-story.html.

This incident underlines the necessity for ongoing training in cultural competency, ethics, and community relations and the implementation of stringent policies and oversight mechanisms to prevent such failures. It also highlights the need for transparency and accountability, ensuring that law enforcement agencies remain aligned with the values and expectations of the society they serve.

Law enforcement agencies must not only enforce the law but also embody the principles of their community, maintaining a standard of conduct that fosters a safe and respectful environment for all. When those standards are compromised, swift and decisive action must be taken to correct the course and restore the bond between the police and the public—a bond that is essential for effective policing.

The dissolution of the Maywood-Cudahy Police Department is not an isolated case; it is part of a broader narrative that has played out across the United States, where the public's trust in and power granted to local law enforcement agencies has been withdrawn due to failures in service or conduct. This phenomenon underscores the fundamental democratic principle that police derive their authority from the consent of the governed—a principle vividly illustrated by events in DeKalb County, Georgia.

In contrast to the disbanding in Maywood-Cudahy, the citizens of DeKalb County took a proactive approach by voting to incorporate the City of Dunwoody on December 1, 2008, breaking away from the DeKalb County government. I was appointed the first police chief on December 17, 2008, and proudly saw the Dunwoody Police Department commence operations on April 1, 2009.

The creation of the City of Dunwoody, and by extension its police department, was driven by citizens' desire for improved services, which extended beyond zoning and infrastructure concerns to encompass the quality of law enforcement provision by DeKalb County. With a local precinct's resources often stretched beyond the city limits, the community felt underserved, spurring them to exercise their power to vote for a change.

The formation of the Dunwoody Police Department stands as a testament to the power of community action and the desire for tailored, localized policing. It reflects the conviction that law enforcement agencies must be attuned to the unique needs of their communities.

The success of the Dunwoody Police Department, as voiced by many citizens, exemplifies a fundamental tenet of community policing:

effective law enforcement is predicated on the respect and trust it garners from the public. To put it plainly, a police force's ability to perform its duties is greatly amplified when it has the support and respect of the community. The story of Dunwoody reaffirms that law enforcement does not just wield the power vested in them by the state but, more importantly, the power granted by the community's endorsement of their presence and practice.

Pivotal events have markedly influenced the fluctuating public perception of law enforcement in recent history. The 1991 Rodney King incident, where excessive force was used by officers and caught on camera, significantly eroded public trust in law enforcement across the nation. In stark contrast, the heroic response of law enforcement to the tragic events of September 11, 2001, served to restore and elevate their status in the eyes of many.

Unfortunately, the deadly shooting of Michael Brown in Ferguson, Missouri, on August 9, 2014, reignited the debate around law enforcement's use of force, particularly in minority communities. The incident sparked widespread protests and civil unrest, leading to intense scrutiny and dialogue on police practices. The subsequent police response, characterized by the use of tear gas and military-grade equipment, was perceived by many as an escalation of violence, exacerbating the already volatile situation and widening the chasm between the community and the police.

These events highlight the importance of context and proportionality in law enforcement's response to community unrest. They underscore the need for ongoing discussions around the use of force, community policing, and racial profiling. The delicate balance between maintaining order and respecting citizens' rights remains a cornerstone of effective policing, and these historical moments serve as stark reminders of the consequences when that balance is lost.

The events in Ferguson in 2014 marked a significant turning point in the public's perception of law enforcement in the United States. The Gallup poll in the same year reflected this shift, revealing that only about half of the American populace reported high confidence in police services. This dramatic decline, registering as the lowest confidence level recorded over two decades, was shocking but predictable. Among African American communities, the trust was markedly lower, with only 30 percent expressing substantial confidence in law enforcement.[12]

This decline in public confidence reflected a growing divide between law enforcement agencies and the communities they serve, particularly in African American communities where the sense of alienation and mistrust was palpable. The statistics from the Gallup poll serve as a barometer of the national sentiment towards police at that time, emphasizing the need for profound changes in law enforcement practices and community engagement.

The impact of such events is not transient; they shape long-term attitudes and influence the relationship dynamics between law enforcement and citizens. In response to this erosion of trust, law enforcement agencies nationwide have been compelled to reassess and often overhaul their community relations strategies, use-of-force policies, and accountability measures.

The shooting of Michael Brown and the subsequent Department of Justice investigation into the Ferguson Police Department significantly impacted national discourse regarding policing and race relations. The Department of Justice's probe, completed in 2015, shed light on deeply concerning issues within the Ferguson Police Department, notably discriminatory practices against African Americans that contravened their constitutional rights.

The report's findings were alarming. It detailed a consistent pattern of unconstitutional policing practices, including stops, searches, and arrests that disproportionately targeted African Americans. Statistics within the report were telling, with African Americans being on the receiving end of nearly 90 percent of use-of-force incidents. These statistics provided stark evidence of a systemic issue of racial bias within the department.[13]

Despite these systemic issues, the investigation did not find evidence to substantiate a civil rights violation by Officer Darren Wilson in the shooting of Michael Brown. The report stated that the available evidence

---

[12]   "Police Confidence in Institutional Practices," Prison Policy Initiative, accessed June 3, 2023, https://www.prisonpolicy.org/blog/2015/07/02/police_confidence/.

[13]   "Justice Department Announces Findings of Two Civil Rights Investigations in Ferguson, Missouri," U.S. Department of Justice, accessed June 3, 2023, https://www.justice.gov/opa/pr/justice-department-announces-findings-two-civil-rights-investigations-ferguson-missouri.

did not corroborate the narrative that Brown had his hands up in surrender when he was shot, nor did it support the claim that Wilson had shot Brown in cold blood. This aspect of the report aligned with the grand jury's decision not to bring an indictment against Wilson.

The Department of Justice's investigation into the Ferguson Police Department, while highlighting significant issues of systemic discrimination, also recognized improvements within the department following the tragic shooting of Michael Brown. Subsequent reforms aimed to address the identified deficiencies and mend the fractured relationship between law enforcement and the Ferguson community.

The report acknowledged new policies and training protocols that the department had instituted, targeting the recruitment of minority officers and educating the existing force on respectful, non-discriminatory community interactions. These steps were vital in shifting the department's culture and practices towards a more inclusive and community-oriented approach.

Additionally, the investigation commended the Ferguson Police Department for effectively handling the ensuing protests and coordinating with neighboring agencies. Such coordination and respect for civil liberties represent a positive departure from the initial heavy-handed tactics that exacerbated tensions.

However, the report also acknowledged the lingering public skepticism and confusion regarding the shooting's actual events. Despite the investigative findings, varying narratives and beliefs persist, demonstrating the complex nature of public perception and the challenges faced in restoring confidence in law enforcement after such polarizing events.

The Department of Justice's investigation into the Ferguson Police Department and the shooting of Michael Brown served as a catalyst for national reflection on police practices and initiated calls for reform across the United States. These events call attention to the imperative for law enforcement agencies to address internal biases, reform policing practices, and rebuild community trust. The report's findings also highlight the complexity of such high-profile cases and the challenges in balancing the pursuit of justice with the need for due process and the rule of law.

The repercussions of the Ferguson incident were felt nationwide, spotlighting law enforcement's relationship with social media. The immediacy with which social media channels like Twitter and Facebook spread news and the ability to share real-time updates, images, and videos has transformed the dynamics of public discourse. Hashtags such as #BlackLivesMatter and #HandsUpDontShoot allowed for a rapid congregation of community sentiment and highlighted the crucial need for timely and transparent communication from law enforcement.

In the aftermath of such incidents, the absence of an immediate, official narrative from the police can cede control of the public discourse to the raw, unfiltered spread of information—or misinformation—on social media. The delay in the Ferguson Police Department's response meant that social media narratives significantly shaped the public's perception, often driven by emotion and incomplete information. This dynamic poses a complex challenge for law enforcement agencies: balancing the urgency of sharing information with the imperative of ensuring its accuracy and completeness.

In today's digital age, the public's respect for police can be significantly influenced by social media's portrayal of events. As a result, law enforcement agencies must adapt to these new communication modalities, ensuring that their perspective is part of the initial information wave following any significant incident. This adaptation is about managing reputations and maintaining public trust, foundational to effective policing and community safety.

In the current landscape, where technological advances and social interconnectivity are at an all-time high, the decline of mutual respect poses a significant challenge to societal harmony. A pervasive disregard for respectful communication is apparent across various platforms, from in-person to digital interactions. The proliferation of derogatory remarks, ad hominem attacks, and a general absence of empathy has become alarmingly common. The art of listening and embracing diverse viewpoints has diminished, leading to polarized communities and a weakened social fabric.

The impact of such a deficit in respect extends beyond personal relationships; it strikes at the core of community trust and collaboration. When respect is sidelined, social ties deteriorate, antagonism rises, and our collective ability to address communal issues is compromised. Institutions need more credibility, and public discourse becomes fraught with conflict, significantly impeding progress.

Highlighting the issue, Deborah Norville points to a concerning trend: Americans appear to be exhibiting increasing rudeness. Surveys indicate that a vast majority—79 percent—view the lack of respect as a severe societal issue.[14] Despite this, it is worth noting that respect is the critical oil that ensures the smooth operation of the intricate machinery of community-police relations. The undercurrent sustains cooperation, understanding, and a shared purpose between law enforcement and the populace they are sworn to protect. Without it, both parties face a tumultuous path forward.

In 2016, Gallup polled the public with the question, *"How much respect do you have for the police in your area – a great deal, some, or hardly any?"*[15] The response was telling of the public sentiment towards law enforcement. An overwhelming 76 percent of those surveyed expressed a great deal of respect for their local police, marking only a one percentage point difference from the historic high of 77 percent in 1967. Conversely, only seven percent reported having 'hardly any' respect.[16]

These statistics reflect a significant improvement in trust and approval for law enforcement among the general populace since Ferguson. Nevertheless, such numbers also punctuate the importance of maintaining high policing standards to preserve and enhance this public trust.

Surprisingly, respect for the police from non-whites was up sharply at 67 percent compared to just 53 percent in 2015. Respect for the police by non-whites is at historic highs.

It is too early to say if this increase in respect can be sustained or the reasons for the sharp increase. Some speculation suggests the rise in respect may have been in response to several high-profile ambush shootings of police officers nationwide.[17] No data supports this conclusion, but it is a reasonable assumption.

After a notable resurgence of respect for the police force in 2016, the nation was again shaken by a tragic incident. On May 25, 2020, George Floyd, an African American man, met a tragic end in Minneapolis,

---

[14] "R-E-S-P-E-C-T: Where Has It Gone?" Today, accessed June 3, 2023, https://www.today.com/popculture/r-e-s-p-e-c-t-where-has-it-wbna33229370.

[15] "Americans' Respect for Police Surges," Gallup, accessed June 3, 2023, https://news.gallup.com/poll/196610/americans-respect-police-surges.aspx?g_source=Politics&g_medium=newsfeed&g_campaign=tiles.

[16] ibid

[17] Ibid

Minnesota. The incident, where a white police officer, Derek Chauvin, was filmed kneeling on Floyd's back for over nine minutes, starkly diminished the previous gains in police respectability. The viral video of Floyd's last moments, where he desperately gasped that he couldn't breathe, became a catalyst for nationwide protests and riots against police brutality.

The ramifications of George Floyd's death were immediate and significant. Public confidence in law enforcement again suffered a substantial blow, with a 2020 Gallup poll indicating that only 48 percent of Americans reported a great deal or quite a lot of confidence in the police—the lowest since the survey's inception in 1993. This incident did not just stir widespread outrage but also reignited an intense debate on systemic racism and the urgent need for comprehensive police reform and enhanced accountability measures.

In the aftermath of Floyd's death, the outcry for justice and transformation within law enforcement was echoed around the globe. The incident became a seminal moment, prompting introspection, dialogues on race relations, and the imperative for a systemic overhaul of policing practices.

In November 2023, the documentary **The Fall of Minneapolis** premiered, casting a new light on the well-known narrative surrounding the death of George Floyd. The film presented a contentious account that challenged widely accepted facts, including the cause of Floyd's death. The documentary aimed to comprehensively examine the events leading up to and following that fateful day, featuring a compilation of interviews, previously unreleased body camera footage, and a review of official documents.[18]

This documentary provoked a fresh wave of debate and analysis. While it offered a perspective that some viewers found compelling, it also ignited controversy, with critics questioning the interpretations and conclusions presented. The documentary's release served as a poignant reminder of the complex nature of such high-profile cases and the ongoing discourse on law enforcement, public perception, and the media's role in shaping narratives.

The release of 'The Fall of Minneapolis' did not simply retell a story; it reignited a conversation about due process, the dissemination of information, and the pursuit of truth in an age of polarized media. It brought attention to

---

[18]   New York Post, "Opinion: Real Truth to Aid the Floyd Lies," accessed November 20, 2023, https://nypost.com/2023/11/20/opinion/real-truth-aid-the-floyd-lies/.

the need for critical thinking and scrutiny as new evidence or perspectives emerge, especially in matters with far-reaching social implications.

Regardless of the exact facts of these incidents, few people can argue that the tragic events involving George Floyd and Michael Brown have significantly impacted the delicate dynamic between law enforcement and various communities, particularly those who feel marginalized. These incidents have not only amplified concerns of disparate treatment and excessive force but have also deepened the chasm of mistrust between the public and the police. Such a divide poses challenges to effective policing, where community cooperation is pivotal for crime prevention and resolution.

These high-profile cases have also imposed an emotional toll on law enforcement personnel. Officers are often subjected to intense scrutiny, leading to heightened stress levels affecting their well-being and operational judgment. A palpable sense of being under siege may pervade, with officers experiencing overt hostility and subtle disrespect during their duties.

In response to these events, there has been a clarion call for sweeping police reforms. The focus has sharpened on enhancing accountability, fostering transparency, and enriching training protocols. While crucial for mending fences with the community, these reforms introduce additional challenges for officers who must now navigate a landscape marked by new rules and expectations.

As we venture into this transformation era, striking a reasonable balance is critical. While it's imperative to hold law enforcement to high standards of conduct and address systemic issues head-on, we must also recognize the majority of officers conduct themselves with honor and integrity. These individuals remain committed to their oath to protect and serve, often under circumstances fraught with complexity and peril. The path toward genuine progress and reconciliation must be charted within this nuanced understanding.

The role of police officers is inherently challenging, a truth that has only become more pronounced in modern times. Officers today must be adept at handling a variety of crimes, easing community tensions, and leveraging new technologies. We must acknowledge the complexities of their duties and provide the necessary support for their welfare, enabling them to serve their communities with distinction.

The ubiquity of recording devices has added a layer of perpetual scrutiny to police work. Not only are officers' actions captured by the public, but also by their body-worn cameras. On the rare occasion when an incident raises questions, footage can circulate on social media, often used to critique law enforcement methods. This relentless examination can be a source of considerable stress.

Consider the immense pressure you would face if every decision and action in your profession were subject to constant scrutiny, with the potential for second-guessing perpetually looming over you.

Imagine being a doctor, where every patient interaction and medical decision is recorded and analyzed. Or envision being a teacher, coach, or any other professional required to wear a body-worn camera to document every conversation and action. This is the daily reality for police officers, who must navigate their duties with the knowledge that their every move is being recorded.

While this level of oversight aims to ensure accountability and transparency, it also contributes to heightened tension in their interactions with the community. The presence of body-worn cameras can serve as both a safeguard and a stressor, adding a layer of complexity to the already challenging role of law enforcement. This constant observation not only impacts the officers' performance but also shapes their relationship with the public as they strive to uphold their duties under the watchful eye of the camera.

Despite these challenges, it's heartening to see that many police departments have fostered strong bonds with their communities. However, this level of trust and mutual respect is not universal. In some areas, achieving this symbiotic relationship is still a work in progress.

Respect is the cornerstone of any healthy relationship, and this holds especially true for the bond between law enforcement and community members. Cultivating respect on both sides can bridge the divides, leading to more effective policing and safer communities.

Each service call is a pivotal moment for police officers—an opportunity to leave a lasting impression, for better or worse, on the individuals they serve. The Dunwoody Police Department lives by the maxim "*Every Call Matters*," approaching every interaction with the utmost importance. They understand that their conduct on each call reflects on themselves, their department, and the law enforcement profession.

The authority granted to law enforcement by communities is not absolute; it is contingent upon the officers' ability to serve with honor and respect. A pattern of disrespect can quickly erode the trust and legitimacy bestowed upon them.

In Sir Robert Peel's time, the repercussions of disrespect might not extend beyond the aggrieved's immediate social circle. A particularly egregious act might garner a mention in the local press, but its impact would be relatively contained.

Today, the landscape is dramatically different. The repercussions of a hostile police encounter ripple outward, resonating through society's collective consciousness. Such incidents can leave deep scars on individuals and erode the fabric of community trust. The pervasive influence of social media amplifies these effects, shaping public perception and dialogue on a national or even global scale.

To mitigate and prevent the far-reaching consequences of these encounters, law enforcement agencies must embrace accountability, transparency, and proactive community outreach. Initiatives that foster open communication, cultivate empathy, and spearhead reform are vital. These efforts can pave the way for a society where law enforcement interactions are infused with trust, dignity, and mutual respect.

When citizens observe their police serving with integrity, they reciprocate with support and endorsement, affirming the officers' actions, behaviors, and commitment to public safety.

Peel's Principles in Practice: Questions for Today's Challenges and Opportunities

Police Officers

1. How is your department ensuring that its policing strategies align with the current values and expectations of the community?
2. What mechanisms are in place to facilitate continual dialogue and feedback between your police department and the community you serve?
3. How is the department measuring the community's trust, and what steps are taken if trust is found to be lacking?
4. What training and development programs are in place within your department to promote cultural competency, ethics, and community relations?
5. How transparent are the department's operations, policies, and decision-making processes to the public?
6. In what ways does your department hold officers accountable for misconduct, and how is this communicated to the community?
7. How does your department respond to incidents of excessive force or violations of civil rights?
8. What efforts are being made to recruit a diverse police force that reflects the community's demographics?
9. How does your department handle the dissemination of information during high-profile incidents to ensure accuracy and mitigate the spread of misinformation?
10. Since the deaths of Michael Brown and George Floyd, has your department conducted a review of critical policies like the use of force?
11. Has your department deployed body-worn cameras?

Citizens

1. How does your police department ensure that its officers understand and respect the community's cultural, racial, and ethnic diversity?
2. What are the procedures for filing complaints against police officers at your department, and how transparent is the investigation process?
3. How accessible are your department's policy manuals, use-of-force guidelines, and training materials
4. How does your department ensure that all community members, especially minorities, feel represented and heard?
5. How does your department measure its success in community policing, and are those metrics publicly available?
6. How are officers trained to de-escalate situations and use force proportionately and appropriately?
7. How does your department handle feedback and criticism from the community, and what mechanisms are in place to implement necessary changes?
8. Are you generally satisfied with the service provided by your local police department?

PRINCIPLE #3

*To recognise always that to secure and maintain the **respect** and **approval** of the public also means ensuring the **willing co-operation** of the public in the task of securing observance of laws.*

Many of Sir Robert Peel's principles are interlinked, creating a foundation that supports and strengthens each one. Respect and approval from the public are not just standalone virtues but are central to law enforcement's ability to function effectively within a society that values democratic principles and the rule of law. This principle emphasizes the necessity of public cooperation, which should not merely be reluctant compliance but a voluntary, active participation in upholding the law.

The distinction between "*willing*" and "*voluntary*" cooperation is subtle yet significant. While willing implies readiness, voluntary suggests a choice without coercion. Both terms underscore the importance of autonomy in the public's decision to observe the law. Indeed, voluntary cooperation can be seen as an implicit aspect of willing cooperation, reflecting a more profound commitment to the law's spirit.

In a democracy, the rule of law is the bedrock upon which order and the protection of rights are built. However, this can only be upheld when the public cooperates with law enforcement. If the community believes law enforcement is inconsistent or is not treating people fairly, cynicism and non-cooperation may fester, undermining society's stability.

Thus, it is imperative for law enforcement to cultivate public respect and approval, which in turn engenders cooperation. This symbiotic relationship hinges on the government's efforts to engage with its citizens transparently and accountably. Open dialogue and clear communication about the laws and their fair application are pivotal to fostering trust.

When the public holds law enforcement in high regard and endorses its actions, they are more inclined to abide by the laws willingly. This respect and approval are not merely desirable but essential for the voluntary cooperation that underpins an effective and humane policing strategy. Without respect and a positive perception of law enforcement, cooperation becomes a product of fear rather than allegiance, a brittle and unsustainable basis for social order.

Law enforcement leaders must, therefore, prioritize nurturing respect and approval from the public to facilitate a cooperative spirit. They must ensure that laws are observed not out of fear but out of a shared commitment to society's welfare and stability.

Securing the willing cooperation of the public is a multifaceted endeavor, wherein procedural justice is a pivotal avenue. This concept is not merely about the outcomes of police interactions but fundamentally concerns the nature of the interactions themselves. Procedural justice is anchored in four core tenets: fairness in the processes, transparency in actions, opportunities for voice, and impartiality in decision-making.[19]

Fairness in processes ensures that the police procedures and methods used when dealing with the public are fair and consistent for everyone. This fairness is the cornerstone of trust and legitimacy; when the public believes that the police treat them fairly, they are more likely to comply with and cooperate with law enforcement.

Transparency in actions means the police are open about their operations and decision-making processes. When the public understands why officers take specific actions, it reduces uncertainty and suspicion, allowing for informed dialogue and contributing to the public's trust in the police.

---

[19]   "Procedural Justice," Community Oriented Policing Services, U.S. Department of Justice, accessed June 3, 2023, https://cops.usdoj.gov/prodceduraljustice.

Providing opportunities for voice is about allowing individuals to speak during encounters with law enforcement. When people feel heard, they perceive the process as more equitable, which enhances their respect for and cooperation with the police.

Impartiality in decision-making requires decisions based on objective criteria rather than personal biases or prejudices. This impartiality assures the community that everyone will be treated equally, regardless of background.

By integrating these principles of Procedural Justice into everyday policing, law enforcement can build a strong foundation of public trust. This trust enables the police to secure the community's willing cooperation.

In practice, procedural justice can manifest in various ways, from community policing initiatives emphasizing collaboration with neighborhood residents to training programs that help officers develop skills to interact more positively with the public. It's about creating and sustaining a dialogue between the police and the community that fosters mutual respect.

Therefore, law enforcement agencies must commit to these principles in policy and practice. Doing so reinforces the public's perception of the police as legitimate, fair, and deserving of cooperation. This perception is integral to the voluntary observance of the law and maintaining public order.

Procedural justice is not just a theoretical concept; it's a practical approach that benefits the community and law enforcement officers. When officers are well-trained and supported to implement fair, transparent, and understandable procedures, they perform their duties more confidently and face fewer conflicts. This approach also reduces the stress officers often experience when uncertain about the appropriate course of action, thereby mitigating the risks of burnout or ethical challenges.

Furthermore, procedural justice strengthens the foundation of a positive work environment within law enforcement agencies. Clear guidelines, robust accountability measures, and a culture that champions fairness and respect enhance officer satisfaction and organizational effectiveness. Officers take pride in their work when they know they are serving the community in a just and equitable manner.

Adherence to the four tenets of procedural justice—fairness, transparency, voice, and impartiality—equips police departments to earn and maintain the public's willing cooperation. This cooperation is fundamental to effective policing and emphasizes the vital role that respect and trust play in the dynamic between law enforcement and citizens.

In essence, procedural justice principles serve as a beacon, guiding law enforcement agencies toward a future where the ethos of policing aligns with the values of the society it aims to protect and serve. When police departments commit to these tenets, they enforce the law, reinforce the social contract, earn public respect, and encourage community collaboration.

Chuck Ramsey, the respected retired police commissioner of the Philadelphia Police Department, often relates a profound story from the early days of his career that exemplifies the essence of procedural justice and the critical nature of treating people with respect.

When Ramsey served as a sergeant in the Chicago Police Department, he had the opportunity to work with an officer named Paris Patton. Patton's ability to de-escalate tense situations during drug raids and his uncanny knack for developing reliable informants were remarkable. Intrigued by Patton's unique capabilities, Ramsey one day inquired about his approach to such challenging aspects of policing.

Patton's response eloquently captured a philosophy of respect and human dignity, articulating a concept later recognized as procedural justice. He said:

"At the moment of birth, every person is a perfect ten. But deduct three right away because life is temporary and doesn't last forever. If you are born into a dysfunctional family where there is substance abuse or domestic violence, deduct another three because the environment you are in will be difficult. You don't have the kind of role model you need, and it will be difficult for you to make it. If you are a member of a minority group, deduct another three because some doors may not be open for you that are open for others. That leaves one. That person's dignity and self-respect. Do what you must do as a police officer, but never, ever do anything to take away that person's dignity and self-respect because that is all they have left, and they will fight you to hold on to it."

These insightful words, spoken over fifty years ago, resonate with the principles of procedural justice long before the term was formally introduced into police training. They remind us that the key to lawful and effective policing lies in maintaining the dignity and self-respect of those we serve.

Chuck Ramsey uses Patton's wisdom to illustrate that policing with procedural justice is not just about following procedures; it's about recognizing the humanity in each individual. This human-centered approach is fundamental to enhancing community perceptions of police legitimacy, rooted in the belief that the police have the moral authority and right to maintain social order.

As law enforcement agencies strive to implement procedurally just practices, they contribute to building a bridge of trust between officers and the communities they protect. By treating every person with the utmost respect and preserving their dignity at every turn, police officers can fortify their role as legitimate and valued protectors of society.

Law enforcement agencies are responsible for conducting themselves with utmost integrity and accountability. It is imperative that any alleged misconduct within these agencies is thoroughly investigated and, if substantiated, addressed with appropriate measures. This commitment to accountability fortifies the public's trust and affirms the government's dedication to the principles of justice and the protection of civil liberties.

Dr. Tom R. Tyler's research provides valuable insights into law enforcement and community cooperation dynamics. His studies reveal that when law enforcement is perceived as legitimate—a belief that the police have the moral authority to maintain social order and enforce laws—communities are more inclined to engage positively with officers, comply with the law, and assist in law enforcement initiatives.[20]

This perception of legitimacy is achieved through just and equitable enforcement of the law and the quality of the officers' interactions with community members. Law enforcement agencies can strengthen this legitimacy by consistently demonstrating fairness, offering opportunities for meaningful community input, making decisions transparently, and treating all individuals with respect and impartiality.

By adhering to these principles, law enforcement not only upholds the rule of law but also nurtures a collaborative partnership with the public, ensuring a more cohesive, safe, and just society.

---

[20] Rosenbaum, Dennis P., ed. "Problem-Oriented Policing: Reflections on the First 20 Years." U.S. Department of Justice, Office of Community Oriented Policing Services, July 1995. Accessed June 3, 2023. https://ric-zai-inc.com/Publications/cops-w0795-pub.pdf.

The dynamics of interaction between law enforcement and the public are pivotal to developing trust and attaining cooperative relationships. The onus of fostering this trust lies significantly in how law enforcement engages with community members. Positive interactions go a long way in establishing a foundation for this trust, thereby greatly enhancing the prospect of willing cooperation from the public.

Yet, it is equally important to acknowledge that building trust is a two-way street. The public also plays a crucial role in this partnership. Community members can significantly aid law enforcement by staying vigilant and reporting suspicious activities or crimes. Through such collaborative efforts, effective policing can thrive, benefiting the entire community.

A visible and responsive police presence, combined with a willingness to address the concerns raised by community members, shapes public perception positively. Witnessing the tangible outcomes of their cooperation can strengthen the community's trust in law enforcement, nurturing a harmonious relationship built on mutual respect and understanding.

Moreover, when individuals assist law enforcement by providing information, they become proactive contributors to the safety and security of their neighborhoods. This act of sharing information not only aids in crime prevention but also fosters a sense of civic duty and community pride.

The role of public cooperation in law enforcement is indeed important. It bolsters the legitimacy of policing, helps to maintain public safety, and deters criminal behavior. Engaging with law enforcement is not just a duty but a shared responsibility that enables a thriving, secure community and highlights the power of collective action in upholding the rule of law.

Community engagement is a critical component of modern policing strategies. It goes beyond the fundamental call to service and encompasses a wide range of activities encouraging public participation in maintaining safety and security. Community policing initiatives are a testament to the power of partnership between the police and the communities they serve.

Active participation in community policing can take various forms. Residents may collaborate with officers to set up neighborhood watch programs, which act as a deterrence to crime and a means to report suspicious activities. Additionally, organizing and participating in community events can strengthen the relationship between the police and the public. Volunteering with the police department allows citizens to contribute directly to crime prevention and gain insight into law enforcement's workings.

The importance of these initiatives is recognized at the national level. The International Association of Chiefs of Police, in partnership with the Bureau of Justice Assistance, Office of Justice Programs, oversees the Volunteers in Police Service (VIP) program. This program exemplifies the commitment to integrating community members into local law enforcement efforts.[21]

The VIP program and similar initiatives across the country demonstrate the variety of ways in which citizens can engage with and support their local police departments. These efforts not only bolster the crime-fighting capabilities of the police but also nurture a spirit of unity and shared purpose. As community members become more involved, they play a pivotal role in shaping the policing strategies that affect their neighborhoods, leading to a more harmonious and cooperative environment for all.

Community involvement in policing, exemplified by the Dunwoody Police Department's use of citizen volunteers, is a testament to the synergistic power of law enforcement and public collaboration. Since its inception in 2009, the department has effectively integrated volunteers into essential roles, initially serving as Court Bailiffs. This innovative approach addressed immediate needs and set the stage for a more extensive community participation program.

In 2016, the department further capitalized on this collaborative spirit by initiating a Citizens on Patrol program, empowering residents to participate in crime prevention actively. These citizen patrols on the streets act as a significant crime deterrent, providing additional surveillance and contributing to a secure community atmosphere.

Citizens on Patrol programs underscore the benefits of community engagement. Volunteers, familiar with the nuances of their neighborhoods, become a vital resource, enhancing the crime prevention capabilities of the police. They serve as a bridge between the police and the community, facilitating faster responses to incidents, which can prevent minor issues from escalating into more significant threats.

---

[21]   International Association of Chiefs of Police (IACP), "Volunteers in Police Service (VIPS)," accessed May 31, 2023, https://www.theiacp.org/projects/volunteers-in-police-service-vips.

Moreover, these volunteers contribute to community education, informing residents about the importance of vigilance and how to report suspicious behavior effectively. This empowerment extends the reach of law enforcement, fostering a culture of shared responsibility for public safety.

The strategic use of community resources through such programs enhances public safety and fosters an environment of mutual respect and understanding. It demonstrates the importance of treating community members fairly and positively impacting the relationship between the police and the public.

As critical as it is to apply these principles in the community, it is equally, if not more, essential to uphold them within law enforcement agencies. Internally, these values contribute to a healthy workplace, reflected in the quality of public service provided. When police departments practice what they preach, the integrity and effectiveness of law enforcement are upheld, and community trust is deepened.

Understanding the profound connection between internal departmental culture and external community relations is crucial for effective law enforcement leadership. Unfortunately, a disconnect in this understanding remains a systemic issue in many police departments. The treatment of law enforcement staff by their agencies and leaders can significantly influence how these officers interact with the public. Respect and proper treatment within the department can lead to a culture of respect and fair treatment in the community.

A toxic internal environment where officers feel undervalued, unheard, or subject to favoritism is often mirrored in their demeanor toward citizens. When officers do not receive the respect they deserve from their ranks, it's unreasonable to expect them to exhibit respect and fairness in their public duties consistently. This is why nurturing a positive workplace culture within law enforcement agencies is not just a matter of internal policy but a critical element of public service.

The consequences of a police force that lacks public respect and approval can be severe. Without the public's trust, the willingness to cooperate with the police diminishes, endangering the very fabric of the rule of law. It's a slippery slope from there to increased lawlessness and societal discord. In contrast, a respected and well-regarded police force is likelier to enjoy the public's cooperation, leading to more effective policing and a safer community.

To maintain the rule of law, law enforcement agencies must strive to build an internal culture of respect, communication, and fairness. This approach should permeate every level of the organization, ensuring officers are supported, valued, and treated equitably. When the workforce feels respected and part of a fair and inclusive culture, they are more likely to extend those same courtesies to the community they serve. The ripple effect of a positive internal culture can be the cornerstone of establishing and maintaining public trust and cooperation.

Imagine a society suddenly devoid of its guardians, the harbingers of order and safety. This scenario came to life in Cordoba, Argentina, a striking example of the critical need for law enforcement and the public's willing cooperation. On December 4, 2013, the majority of Cordoba's police force went on strike, and with only a fraction of officers reporting for duty, the city was left virtually unprotected.

The consequences were immediate and severe. The absence of a police presence emboldened criminals, who swiftly capitalized on the situation. Reports from that time describe a wave of looting and burglary, with mobs targeting electronics stores and liquor outlets, stripping them of their goods. This lack of police is a stark reminder of the fine line between order and chaos.[22]

Cordoba, Argentina's second-largest city, is typically a bustling urban center, relying on its contingent of 600 police officers to maintain law and order. However, during the strike, with a mere 10% of its force on duty, the city experienced firsthand the vacuum created by the absence of law enforcement.

In the disquieting silence of the police strike, a grim narrative unfolded. The law-abiding citizens, confronted with unchecked lawlessness, found themselves at a crossroads between order and vigilante justice. In one disturbing incident, the frustration and fear gripping the city culminated in a group of citizens fatally assaulting a looter. This tragedy underscores the perils of a society teetering on the brink of disorder, where the line between self-protection and vigilantism becomes dangerously blurred.

---

[22]   Virginia Castiglione, "Chaos and Social Unrest: A Night Without the Police in Cordoba, Argentina," Thought Catalog, January 2014, accessed June 3, 2023, https://thoughtcatalog.com/virginia-castiglione/2014/01/chaos-and-social-unrest-a-night-without-the-police-in-cordoba-argentina/.

The Cordoba experience highlights the vital role that police officers play in society, not only in their active duty but also in the symbolic weight of their presence. The police strike led to a breakdown in societal norms and a window into what could occur without the thin blue line that separates civilization from anarchy.

Examining the relationship between law enforcement and the communities they serve is crucial, considering the Cordoba crisis. As Sir Robert Peel stated in this principle, the willing cooperation of the public with the police is a cornerstone of modern policing. It is a symbiotic relationship; the police are as reliant on public support and cooperation as the public is on police protection and service.

This episode also illuminates the importance of addressing the concerns and needs of law enforcement personnel. When the police feel unsupported or undervalued, the repercussions can be felt community-wide. It is a sobering lesson in ensuring that those tasked with upholding the law are supported, respected, and equipped to perform their duties, thereby preventing such crises.

As law enforcement agencies analyze the lessons from Cordoba, it becomes clear that investing in the police force is not merely a matter of funding or resources; it is about ensuring stability, safety, and the upkeep of societal values. This strike is a clarion call for proactive engagement, respect, and mutual support between the public and the police, forming a united front against the forces of disorder.

The strike's aftermath left a city grappling with the consequences of its vulnerability, a stark example of the interdependence of law enforcement and civil society. The chaos in Cordoba was a catalyst for change, an imperative for all stakeholders to reevaluate the systems that underpin public safety and the treatment of those who enforce it.

The governor's swift action in negotiating a resolution was pivotal in quelling the unrest and reinstating a semblance of normalcy. The return of the police force to their duties was a profound relief to the besieged city and a reminder of the fundamental role that law enforcement plays in safeguarding society.

As communities teeter on the precipice of unrest, a single spark—a misjudgment, an error, a misunderstanding—could set off a chain reaction of distrust and noncompliance with law enforcement, propelling society toward chaos. This delicate balance is a constant reminder of the fragility of public order and the imperative need for every interaction between police and citizens to be handled with care.

The cornerstone of citizens' compliance during police encounters is the mutual desire to preserve safety and uphold the sanctity of community well-being. Officers are adept at navigating the complexities of public safety and are trained to defuse volatile situations while safeguarding all involved. Compliance is an act of surrender and a proactive measure to ensure collective security.

Trust is the lifeblood of the police-community partnership. When citizens extend their cooperation, law enforcement can perform their duties with effectiveness and discretion. This synergy is critical in deterring crime, reducing conflict, and enabling a focus on more pressing security challenges.

Beyond the immediacy of any police encounter lies the overarching framework of accountability and due process. Compliance does not negate the right to recourse; it sets the stage for it. Through established channels and with respect for the procedures in place, individuals can seek justice and hold law enforcement to the highest standards of conduct.

In sum, willing cooperation with law enforcement is a multifaceted act that reinforces safety, respects the law, enhances effective policing, and ensures accountability. It is a cornerstone of civility, a marker of a society that values order, justice, and the collective good.

The fracturing of trust and cooperation in Ferguson, Missouri, following the fatal shooting of Michael Brown by Officer Darren Wilson, is a quintessential example of the fragility of community-police relations. The ensuing protests, riots, and overall disregard for the rule of law were symptoms of a deeper malaise—a long-standing disconnect between the Ferguson Police Department and the community it served.

The events in Ferguson were a litmus test, revealing the consequences when respect and approval erode between citizens and law enforcement. The tumultuous aftermath was not merely about a single incident but a testament to the cumulative impact of perceived and real injustices over time.

This cautionary tale emphasizes the importance of every police interaction. Departments must recognize that each encounter can either build or erode the community's trust. Policing must transcend the transactional nature of law enforcement to embody principles of dignity, respect, and impartiality.

The lessons from Ferguson and similar incidents across the country echo the critical need for continuous engagement and dialogue between law enforcement and communities. Positive interactions between police and citizens are quickly overshadowed by conflict, making it imperative for departments to cultivate solid and ongoing relationships with the public.

It is clear—every police action, every conversation, every response to a call for help—contributes to the narrative of policing. When officers conduct themselves with integrity and treat individuals respectfully, they lay the foundation for willing cooperation and observance of the law.

How officers engage with individuals during police encounters can significantly influence public sentiment. Positive or negative, the perception of treatment often resonates more deeply than the actual outcome of the encounter. It is in the hands of law enforcement to ensure that each interaction reinforces the pillars of trust, approval, and respect that are vital for a harmonious society.

Peel's Principles in Practice: Questions for Today's Challenges and Opportunities

Police Officers

1. How is your department implementing the four core tenets of Procedural Justice: fairness, transparency, voice, and impartiality?
2. How does your department ensure that every individual feels heard and respected during interactions with law enforcement, as emphasized by Officer Paris Patton's philosophy?
3. What internal policies does your department have that support officers in making decisions free from personal biases or prejudices?
4. In what ways does your department seek to cultivate public respect and approval to enhance voluntary cooperation, as indicated by the principle laid out by Sir Robert Peel?
5. Can you identify concrete examples of your department's engagement and communication efforts directly increasing public trust and cooperation?
6. How is your department training officers to uphold every individual's dignity and self-respect?
7. How does your department address and publicly report on misconduct allegations to maintain accountability and public trust?
8. Has your department provided training in procedural justice to all employees?

Citizens

1. How does your police department facilitate community members' voices being heard in law enforcement interactions?
2. What steps has your department taken to prevent bias and ensure impartiality in their dealings with the community?
3. How does your department measure and seek public approval, and what forums are available for community feedback?
4. In what ways can citizens participate in community policing initiatives, and what has been the impact of such participation?
5. How does your police department demonstrate its commitment to respecting individual dignity and self-respect in its interactions?
6. How are the principles of Procedural Justice reflected in the day-to-day actions of your local police department, and how can citizens learn more about these principles?
7. Do you volunteer at your local police department?

PRINCIPLE #4

*To recognise always that the extent to which the co-operation of the public can be secured **diminishes** proportionately the necessity of the use of physical force and **compulsion** for achieving police objectives.*

This principle encapsulates a profound understanding that was as visionary in Sir Robert Peel's time as it is today. It asserts that effective law enforcement requires the willing cooperation of the public, predicated not on force or fear but on a shared sense of justice and communal responsibility.

Policing in Peel's era bore little resemblance to modern policing. There were no professional standards for hiring officers; connections trumped competence. The absence of technology and formal training meant officers frequently resorted to brute force rather than community policing or problem-solving strategies.

The "*tough street cop*" persona, a mythologized figure in law enforcement lore, was often glorified for handling issues with physical strength rather than prudence or tact.[23] This archetype, however, is not sustainable or desirable in modern society, where the relationship between the police and the public is under intense scrutiny.

The reliance on brute force as a primary tool for law enforcement, which marked much of early policing history, often led to excesses that were noticed and recognized even in those times. A poignant illustration of this is the Police with Pistols editorial from the New York Times published on November 15, 1858, which expressed grave concerns over using deadly force in the pursuit of suspects.

"The pistols are not used in self-defense," the editorial noted, *"but to stop the men who are running away. They are considered substitutes for swift feet and long arms. Now, we doubt the propriety of employing them for such a purpose. A Policeman has no right to shoot a man for running away from him. But what right have Policemen to carry revolvers at all? We doubt very much the policy of arming our Policemen with revolvers."*

This apprehension about arming police officers reflects a long-standing debate about the balance between maintaining public order and preserving individual rights. As the editorial suggests, the threshold for using lethal force should be high and reserved for situations where there is an immediate threat to life or serious bodily harm. The concept of shooting a suspect merely for fleeing was—and remains—a profoundly troubling notion, highlighting the critical need for restraint and accountability in policing.

The rapid resort to force continued into the 20th century, with law enforcement often operating with scant consideration for the communities they served. This history reminds us of the necessity of having modern standards that emphasize de-escalation, community engagement, and proportional use of force. It also illustrates the complex evolution of policing and the enduring need to reconcile law enforcement's imperatives with individuals' rights and dignity.

Modern law enforcement understands that using force is a critical tool that must be applied judiciously, proportionately, and crucially, with impartiality. Only under these conditions can the public's trust be won,

---

[23] "English and American policing in the late 19th century," Encyclopedia Britannica, accessed June 3, 2023, https://www.britannica.com/topic/police/English-and-American-policing-in-the-late-19th-century.

and their cooperation secured. Without public approval and voluntary compliance, the alternative is a bleak landscape where lawlessness and disorder thrive, threatening the very fabric of society.

A gradual but steady shift towards professionalism, accountability, and a commitment to community engagement has marked the evolution of policing from Peel's time to the present day. This progress is vital to maintain, especially in turbulent times, where each act of policing can either fortify or fracture the delicate trust between citizens and those sworn to protect them.

As we move forward, the law enforcement community must continue to embody the spirit of this principle, recognizing that each interaction with the public is a chance to reinforce or erode the foundations of cooperation and respect essential for the rule of law to prevail.

In 1929, under the leadership of President Herbert Hoover, the National Commission on Law Observance and Enforcement, commonly known as the Wickersham Commission, was established to conduct an unprecedented inquiry into crime and law enforcement in the United States. The societal effects of Prohibition provided the impetus for this comprehensive review.

The Commission's extensive findings, published across fourteen volumes in 1931 and 1932, provided a broad and often damning picture of American criminal justice. One volume, titled Lawlessness in Law Enforcement, particularly resonated with the American public. The report within this volume exposed and decried the pervasive use of the *"third degree"*—a term denoting the practice where police officers subjected suspects to various forms of physical and psychological coercion to extract confessions or information.[24]

The revelation of such practices brought attention to the grim reality: individuals supposed to protect the public and uphold the law sometimes resort to unlawful methods. These methods contradicted the principles of justice and often resulted in false confessions and miscarriages of justice.

The Wickersham Commission's work exposed the need for reform in law enforcement practices, highlighting the imperative for due process and the humane treatment of suspects. It was a clarion call for procedural

---

[24]   "Wickersham Commission," JRank Law Encyclopedia, accessed June 3, 2023, https://law.jrank.org/pages/11309/Wickersham-Commission.html.

fairness and ethical conduct within policing, and this call resonates as foundational in contemporary discussions about law enforcement and its role in society.

The legacy of the Wickersham Commission reminds us of the ongoing challenge of ensuring that law enforcement operates within the bounds of law and justice. It remains a touchstone for examining how far the criminal justice system has come and the work that still lies ahead to maintain the delicate balance between enforcing the law and protecting civil liberties.

The call for professionalization within law enforcement was a cornerstone of the Commission's reforms. By advocating for established training programs, standardized procedures, and clear career paths, the Commission sought to enhance the quality of policing and reduce the likelihood of corruption. Such professionalization would result in a more competent and conscientious police force.

The recommendation to form a national coordinating body for law enforcement anticipated the need for a unified approach to crime fighting. The establishment of the Federal Bureau of Investigation, an outcome influenced by the Commission's work, was a direct response to the need for better coordination and the application of advanced investigative techniques across states.

Community relations were another area of focus. The Commission recognized that trust between law enforcement and the public was paramount to the effectiveness of policing. Trust-building was seen as a pathway to better policing and lower crime rates.

Standardization of procedures was recommended to ensure uniformity and fairness in policing. The Commission foresaw that such measures would reduce errors and prevent misconduct, thereby bolstering the integrity of law enforcement.

The embrace of modern technology was a forward-looking recommendation by the Commission. Using fingerprinting and polygraphs and establishing crime laboratories were anticipated to revolutionize criminal investigations, increasing efficiency and accuracy.

Regarding police management, the Commission suggested merit-based promotion systems and performance evaluations. These recommendations aimed to shield law enforcement from political influences, ensuring that police work remained focused on safety and justice rather than political expediency.

Finally, the Commission emphasized the importance of community involvement in crime prevention. The recommendation was rooted in the belief that an engaged public would enhance safety and reduce crime. Community involvement was seen as a force multiplier, extending the reach and impact of law enforcement efforts.

The Wickersham Commission's recommendations were a blueprint for reform that laid the groundwork for modern law enforcement practices. While not all recommendations were adopted as proposed, the Commission's report remains a seminal document in the history of American policing, embodying principles that continue to underpin efforts to advance the professionalism and effectiveness of law enforcement.

Ironically, the commission reported the chief evil as the short-term service of the police chief and the chief being controlled by politicians.[25]

Following the Wickersham Commission's influential work, the Kerner Commission was established to delve deeper into the issues facing law enforcement and their relationship with the community, especially in the wake of civil unrest:

The Kerner Commission, established during significant social strife in the United States, was tasked with dissecting the complex causes of civil unrest. In its pursuit, the Commission unearthed systemic failings that transcended the immediate sphere of law enforcement, reaching into the broader domains of social policy.

The Kerner Report, released in 1968, was a bleak reminder to the nation. It revealed the profound impact of entrenched socio-economic disparities and the government's role in perpetuating these conditions. It laid bare the inadequacies in education, housing, and social services that contributed to the volatile environment of the time.[26] These failures led to riots across the country.

This report expanded the conversation on policing by framing law enforcement within the larger context of institutional responsibility. It highlighted the intricate interplay between societal conditions and the role

---

[25]   "Wickersham Report on Police." *The American Journal of Police Science* 2, no. 4 (1931): 337–48. https://doi.org/10.2307/1147362.

[26]   "Kerner Commission," Wikipedia, accessed June 3, 2023, https://en.wikipedia.org/wiki/Kerner_Commission.

of law enforcement, suggesting that effective policing could not be siloed from the socio-economic realities of the communities they serve.

The Kerner Commission's findings underscored the necessity for a more integrated approach to governance that could address the root causes of discontent and disenfranchisement that often lead to civil unrest. It recognized that without a concerted effort to improve the foundational aspects of society, such as education and housing, any improvements in policing would likely be insufficient in creating lasting peace and justice.

The report was a call to action for policymakers and law enforcement agencies to reconsider their strategies and engage with communities meaningfully and empathetically. By doing so, it aimed to foster an environment where trust and cooperation could flourish, and law enforcement could be seen not as an imposing force but as a supportive pillar within the community.

One of the Kerner Commission's findings, **The Challenge of Crime in a Free Society**, brought forth a nuanced critique of law enforcement's handling of the riots that swept across various American cities. The report pointed to a pattern of excessive force, which tragically resulted in the loss of lives and further deepened the chasm between the police and the communities they were meant to serve.[27]

This examination of police action during the riots revealed a concerning reflex towards an overzealous response. It illuminates the urgent need for restraint and a calibrated approach to managing large-scale public disturbances. The Commission's findings suggested that the deaths could have been mitigated had a more measured and community-centric strategy been implemented.

The implications of these findings were far-reaching. They called for a reevaluation of police protocols in riot control and engagement with civil unrest. They underscored the importance of balancing the preservation of order with respect for individual rights and the sanctity of life.

The report catalyzed a broader discourse on the role of police in a democratic society, emphasizing the concept of *"policing by consent"* rather

[27] "The 1968 Kerner Commission Got It Right, But Nobody Listened," Smithsonian Magazine, accessed June 3, 2023, https://www.smithsonianmag.com/smithsonian-institution/1968-kerner-commission-got-it-right-nobody-listened-180968318/.

than by force. It advocated for a policing model that prioritized democratic principles, such as transparency, accountability, and respect for civil liberties, over an authoritarian stance.

The Challenge of Crime in a Free Society initiated reforms within law enforcement agencies, prompting introspection and subsequent adoption of policies that aimed to professionalize the police force. These reforms included enhanced training for riot control, improved community relations, and the integration of less lethal methods of crowd management.

Central to the Commission's recommendations was the adoption of community policing models. The Commission urged that officers embed themselves within the communities they patrol, fostering relationships that could lead to collaborative efforts in crime prevention and a deeper mutual understanding. This approach sought to replace adversarial interactions with partnerships, reshaping the police force into a community-centric entity.

The Commission also addressed the homogeneity within the ranks of law enforcement. It highlighted the urgent need for diversity, advocating for recruiting officers who mirror the rich mosaic of the community. This diversity would enhance cultural competence and engender a sense of representation and inclusivity, potentially bridging the gap between different community segments and the police.

Training was pinpointed as a crucial lever for improvement. The Commission stressed that officers must receive comprehensive cultural awareness and conflict de-escalation instruction. Mastery in these areas could reduce violent confrontations, foster peaceful resolutions, and preserve lives.

Furthermore, the Kerner Commission stressed the necessity of accountability mechanisms in the form of civilian review boards. Empowering citizens with the ability to review and influence police conduct would instill a system of checks and balances, nurturing trust through transparency and decency.

One focus of the report was related to the use of civilian review boards.

The discourse surrounding Civilian Review Boards (CRBs) has taken center stage in national conversations about police oversight and accountability. Especially in the wake of high-profile incidents, many advocate for establishing or strengthening CRBs to increase transparency and trust in law enforcement.

CRBs, when effectively implemented, are designed to provide oversight of police actions from a civilian standpoint, separate from the internal dynamics of a police department. They can take various forms and have differing levels of authority. Still, their core mission typically involves examining and reviewing complaints against police officers and, in some instances, broader policy issues within the department.

The scope of a CRB's responsibilities can vary widely. In some cities, boards are granted significant investigatory powers, including the ability to subpoena witnesses and review police department policies. In others, their role is more advisory, providing recommendations to the police department or city officials based on their findings. This variance often leads to discussions about the usefullness of such boards, with some arguing that without substantial investigative powers and independence from the police department, CRBs cannot effectively serve their purpose.[28]

Moreover, the structure of CRBs can impact their effectiveness. Some are composed of diverse community members, while others include legal experts, former law enforcement officers, or civil rights advocates. The composition of these boards often reflects the community's values and the specific issues of police-community relations they aim to address.

The establishment of CRBs is sometimes met with resistance from police unions and some community members who question their impact on policing effectiveness and the potential for overreach. Conversely, proponents argue that CRBs are essential to ensuring police are accountable to the communities they serve.

In large cities, where police-community relations are often under the microscope, CRBs have become a focal point for efforts to reform policing practices. Their presence is seen as a commitment to upholding the principles of justice and due process, ensuring that those entrusted with enforcing the law are also bound by it.

The effectiveness of CRBs continues to be a topic of vigorous debate, with each incident of alleged police misconduct bringing renewed attention to their role in maintaining the delicate balance between effective law enforcement and the public's civil liberties. As this debate continues, it becomes clear that the call for CRBs is not just about oversight but also

---

28   American Police Beat, "Citizen Review Boards versus Citizen Advisory Boards," accessed August 31, 2023, https://apbweb.com/2023/08/citizen-review-boards-versus-citizen-advisory-boards/.

about the community's desire for a voice in how they are policed and a say in the standards to which their police officers are held.

The debate around implementing Civilian Review Boards (CRBs) versus the alternative of Civilian Advisory Boards (CABs) is a nuanced aspect of the broader discussion on police accountability and community relations. Proponents of CRBs and CABs argue that these entities provide essential oversight of police actions, bringing an independent civilian perspective to issues of misconduct and policy.

Critics, however, often claim that the existence of elected officials within city councils or commissions negates the need for an additional layer of review, positing that these elected bodies should suffice in oversight given their representative nature.

From this standpoint, the contention against CRBs is rooted in concerns over bureaucratic redundancy, the potential for conflicting authority, and the ability of such boards to produce tangible outcomes.

On the other hand, the concept of a CAB presents a different approach. Compared to CRBs, which often have investigatory and disciplinary powers, CABs typically function as liaisons between the police department and the community. They offer a platform for dialogue, policy suggestions, and community engagement without the formal oversight powers attributed to CRBs.[29]

Some see this collaborative model as a less aggressive means of building trust and fostering communication between law enforcement and citizens. The advisory nature of CABs means they can work on a range of community concerns, from public safety strategies to youth outreach, without directly challenging the police department's authority.

CABs can influence police policies and strategies by allowing community priorities and concerns to be heard. However, the lack of formal oversight authority may limit their ability to hold departments accountable like CRBs aim to do. This limitation is often a disadvantage for those who advocate for robust civilian oversight mechanisms that can enact disciplinary measures or policy changes.

The discussion around CRBs and CABs ultimately reflects the community's desires regarding police oversight. While some communities may favor the direct oversight and investigatory powers of CRBs, others

---

[29]   ibid

might prefer the advisory and collaborative approach of CABs, seeking to influence rather than directly control police policies and actions. The decision between the two models reflects a balance of accountability, trust, and the level of involvement the community desires in their police department's operations.

Lastly, the Kerner Commission's call for increased federal funding to bolster police departments, especially in underserved communities, underscores a persistent issue in law enforcement: the need for adequate resources to ensure effective community policing. The commission recognized that the lack of investment in specific communities was a significant contributor to the friction between police and residents. Financial support aimed at improving policing practices promised to enhance law enforcement capabilities and alleviate tensions by fostering better community relations.

However, the partial adoption of the commission's recommendations has been a critical factor in the ongoing dialogue about police reform. Despite progress in some areas, such as the adoption of community policing models and the establishment of some form of civilian oversight, the full vision of the commission has yet to be realized. High-profile cases of police brutality have reignited discussions on the use of force and the urgent need for substantial reform.

Efforts to diversify police forces have seen some success, acknowledging that representation matters and can positively influence community interactions. Recruitment drives and diversity training aim to create a force that more accurately reflects the community's demographics, potentially reducing racial tensions and improving cultural competence among officers.

The implementation challenge, as noted, remains intricately tied to funding. The commission's vision of a well-resourced police force equipped to handle its duties effectively is hindered by financial constraints, which also affect social services that could mitigate some of the underlying issues contributing to crime and unrest. The ongoing debate on reallocating funds within and beyond law enforcement reflects a broader societal struggle to balance immediate safety needs with long-term social investments.

The legacy of the Kerner Commission's findings is a reminder of the complexities of police reform. It highlights the interplay between resource allocation, social equity, and the essential nature of law enforcement's relationship with the communities they serve. The commission's work suggests that for police reform to be genuinely effective, it must be accompanied by a commitment to addressing broader social challenges through sustained investment and community engagement.

In the context of today's complex societal fabric, the essence of the report continues to resonate. It serves as a historical marker for the evolution of policing practices and a reminder of the continuing journey towards a law enforcement paradigm that upholds the rights and dignity of all citizens.

The establishment of various justice assistance and research programs in the wake of the Kerner and Wickersham Commissions indicates a significant shift towards a more scientific and community-focused approach to law enforcement in the United States. These programs were designed to address the complex nature of crime and the necessity for a collaborative relationship between the community and law enforcement.

The creation of the Bureau of Justice Assistance and similar entities provided much-needed support and resources for law enforcement agencies, facilitating improvements in areas such as crime victimization surveys, emergency response systems like 9-1-1, and community policing initiatives. These efforts represent a concerted attempt to modernize police services and enhance their efficiency and effectiveness.

In addition to these initiatives, developing the National Institute of Justice and the Office of Justice Programs has been pivotal in promoting research and development in criminal justice. These institutions foster innovation in crime prevention and control strategies, ensuring that the latest knowledge and technology inform law enforcement practices.

Let's fast forward to 2014, when President Obama established The President's Task Force on 21st Century Policing, appointing 11 members.[30] In May 2015, the Final Report of the President's Task Force on 21st Century Policing was released. The Final Report contained 59 recommendations covering these six pillars, "Building Trust and Legitimacy," "Policy and Oversight," "Technology and Social Media," "Community Policing

---

[30] The White House, Office of the Press Secretary, "President Obama Announces Task Force on 21st Century Policing," December 18, 2014, accessed May 31, 2023, https://obamawhitehouse.archives.gov/the-press-office/2014/12/18/president-obama-announces-task-force-21st-century-policing.

and Crime Reduction," "Officer Training and Education," and "Officer Safety and Wellness."[31]

Although many law enforcement agencies nationwide implemented many of the recommendations contained in the Final Report, it is clear more needs to be done.

On October 28, 2019, President Trump directed Attorney General William Barr to form a Commission to explore modern issues affecting law enforcement's ability to reduce crime.[32]

Attorney General Barr then established the Presidential Commission on Law Enforcement and the Administration of Justice in 2020, appointing 18 Commissioners.[33] I was honored to be appointed as a Subject Matter Expert to the Law Enforcement Recruitment and Training committee.

Regrettably, the advent of COVID-19 significantly disrupted the operations of the Commission and its subcommittees. This unprecedented global health crisis necessitated a swift pivot to virtual platforms, resulting in the majority of the Commission's meetings being conducted remotely. Despite these challenges, the Commission persevered in its mandate, culminating in the publication of the Final Report at the close of 2020.[34]

The comprehensive report presented an array of 170 thoughtfully crafted recommendations, encompassing a broad spectrum of issues pertinent to the Commission's scope.[35] Regrettably, the uptake of these recom-

---

[31]   Office of Justice Programs (OJP), "Final Report of the President's Task Force on 21st Century Policing," accessed May 31, 2023, https://www.ojp.gov/ncjrs/ virtual-library/abstracts/final-report-presidents-task-force-21st-century-policing.

[32]   U.S. Department of Justice, "Attorney General William P. Barr Announces Establishment of Presidential Commission on Law Enforcement and the Administration of Justice," accessed May 31, 2023, https://www.justice.gov/ opa/pr/attorney-general-william-p-barr-announces-establishment-presidential- commission-law.

[33]   ibid

[34]   U.S. Department of Justice, "Presidential Commission on Law Enforcement and the Administration of Justice Releases Final Report," accessed May 31, 2023, https://www.justice.gov/opa/pr/presidential-commission-law-enforcement-and- administration-justice-releases-final-report.

[35]   The Hill, "Trump-created Commission Offers Recommendations on Police," accessed May 31, 2023, https://thehill.com/homenews/administration/532436- trump-created-commission-offers-recommendations-on-police/.

mendations was stymied by a confluence of factors, most notably political dynamics, which unjustly relegated the report to the sidelines. This was a disheartening outcome, especially considering that nestled within the report were recommendations of substantial merit that, if implemented, had the potential to effectuate significant positive change.

While these various commissions have focused on broad strategies for improving law enforcement, one critical area that continually emerges in their findings is the contentious issue of police use of force, which has led to numerous court cases.

The judicial clarification, on police use of force, as illustrated by the 1973 **Johnson v. Glick** case, set a precedent for evaluating the appropriateness of force by law enforcement officers. The four-part test established by this case provided a framework for assessing the necessity and extent of force used, considering the intention behind its application and its consequences.[36] The four-part test is as follows:

1. The need for the application of force.
2. The relationship between the need and the amount of force that was used.
3. The extent of the injury inflicted.
4. Whether force was applied in a good faith effort to maintain or restore discipline or maliciously and sadistically for the very purpose of causing harm.

This legal framework aims to balance officers' need to maintain order and protect themselves with the rights and well-being of individuals in custody. It recognizes the principle that while force may be necessary in certain situations, it must be proportional, reasonable, and intended to uphold discipline rather than inflict harm.

The **Tennessee v. Garner** decision by the Supreme Court in 1985 represented a landmark ruling that significantly reformed the use of deadly force by police in the United States. Before this case, many jurisdictions permitted law enforcement officers to use any means necessary, including

---

[36] "Teaching the New Constitutional Pre-Trial Detainee Standard," Daigle Law Group, accessed June 3, 2023, https://daiglelawgroup.com/wp-content/uploads/2016/10/Teaching-the-New-Consitutional-Pre-Trial-Detainee-Standard.pdf.

lethal force, to apprehend a suspected felon, even if the suspect posed no immediate threat to the officer or others.[37]

The Supreme Court's decision in Tennessee v. Garner set a new constitutional standard, holding that the use of deadly force against a fleeing suspect is a seizure under the Fourth Amendment. Consequently, such force must be reasonable, and the Court declared that the mere fact that a suspect is fleeing does not justify using deadly force. Instead, an officer must have probable cause to believe that the suspect poses a significant threat of death or serious physical injury to the officer or others.

This decision reflected a shift towards more restrictive and accountable police practices, emphasizing the preservation of life and the principle of using the least amount of force necessary. The ruling required law enforcement agencies nationwide to revise their policies and training programs to align with this constitutional mandate. It emphasized deadly force should only be an option when there is an immediate and clear danger, thus promoting the value of human life and the responsible use of police authority.

The **Graham v. Connor** Supreme Court decision in 1989 marked another significant advancement in the legal framework governing police conduct in the United States. This Supreme Court ruling established that the appropriateness of an officer's use of force must be judged through the lens of the Fourth Amendment's *"objective reasonableness"* standard rather than the more subjective standards set by, the earlier Johnson v. Glick test, which considered the officer's intent.[38]

The Court's decision clarified that in determining whether the force used was excessive, one must consider the perspective of a reasonable officer on the scene rather than with the 20/20 vision of hindsight. This means that the court should consider that police officers are often required to make split-second judgments about the amount of force necessary in a particular situation.

---

[37]   "The Legality of Informational Stops: A Study of Federal District Court Decisions," Journal of Criminal Law & Criminology, Northwestern University School of Law, accessed June 3, 2023, https://scholarlycommons.law.northwestern.edu/cgi/viewcontent.cgi?article=6811&context=jclc.

[38]   "Graham v. Connor Court Case," ThoughtCo, accessed June 3, 2023, https://www.thoughtco.com/graham-v-connor-court-case-4172484.

The Graham v. Connor case shifted the focus to the reasonableness of the particular use of force, considering the following factors:

1. The severity of the crime at issue;
2. Whether the suspect poses an immediate threat to the safety of the officers or others; and
3. Whether (the suspect) is actively resisting arrest or attempting to evade arrest by flight.

By establishing this standard, the Supreme Court intended to balance the individual's right to be free from excessive physical force with the community's interest in granting law enforcement certain immunities for making on-the-spot decisions in tense, uncertain, and rapidly evolving situations.

In essence, the ruling recognizes that police officers are often forced to make critical decisions in dynamic and unpredictable circumstances, and it seeks to evaluate their actions based on what they know at the moment rather than on information that comes to light after the fact. This objective standard continues to be applied in cases of alleged excessive force, shaping both legal evaluations of police behavior and the policies guiding law enforcement agencies nationwide.

Since Graham v. Conner, the US Supreme Court and other courts have made additional rulings related to the use of force, but Graham v. Conner is still the standard today, at least for now.

As previously mentioned, the shooting of Michael Brown and the subsequent events in Ferguson, Missouri, represents a pivotal moment in American history, highlighting deep-seated issues regarding police use of force, particularly in African American communities. This incident highlighted the importance of the relationship between law enforcement and the communities they serve, and it sparked a national conversation about race, justice, and policing in America.

Despite Officer Darren Wilson being cleared of wrongdoing by the Department of Justice, the incident left an indelible mark on the collective consciousness of the nation and remains a focus of discussions on policing and racial justice.[39] It highlights the complex interplay between the legal

---

[39] "Darren Wilson Is Cleared of Rights Violations in Ferguson Shooting," The New York Times, accessed June 3, 2023, https://www.nytimes.com/2015/03/05/us/darren-wilson-is-cleared-of-rights-violations-in-ferguson-shooting.html.

justifications of the use of force and the public's perception of that force. Even when an officer's actions are deemed legally justified, there can be a significant public outcry if those actions are not also perceived as fair or necessary by the community.

The Ferguson incident catalyzed a movement that called for widespread reforms in policing, including the adoption of body-worn cameras by police, changes in police training and tactics, more robust community policing efforts, and increased accountability for police misconduct.

This case also illustrates the enduring relevance of the Supreme Court's decision in Graham v. Connor, as each use of force incident is evaluated through objective reasonableness. However, it also highlights that the court's standard is just one element of a broader societal conversation about law enforcement, community relations, and the fair administration of justice.

The Michael Brown shooting in Ferguson dramatically demonstrated the profound impact that public perception and social media can have on the narrative surrounding police use of force. It is a stark reminder of how quickly information — and misinformation — can spread in the digital age, outpacing official accounts and shaping public opinion.

The Ferguson incident also highlights the challenges law enforcement faces in managing public relations and maintaining legitimacy due to controversial events. The delay in the Ferguson Police Department's response allowed the narrative to form without their input, which can create a disconnect between public perception and the facts as determined by subsequent investigations.

The first press conference wasn't held until almost 24 hours after the shooting. By then, thousands and thousands of tweets were posted, establishing the narrative about what happened, and the perceived illegitimacy of the force used by the police.

The role of technology in documenting interactions between police and the public cannot be overstated. While there was no video of the Michael Brown shooting, the incident illuminated the necessity for law enforcement agencies to adopt technologies like body-worn cameras. These tools provide transparency and accountability and serve as an objective record that can corroborate officers' accounts of events or provide evidence of misconduct.

Looking back at the Rodney King incident, it's clear that the intro-duction of the camcorder into the public domain began a new era in police accountability. Now, with smartphones ubiquitous, every citizen has the potential to document and broadcast real-time interactions with law enforcement. This democratization of surveillance has given rise to a new form of public oversight but also presents new challenges for police.

In light of these developments, law enforcement agencies must rec-ognize the power of social media and the speed at which narratives are established. They must engage proactively with the community and media to provide timely and transparent information. Additionally, law enforce-ment must work to build relationships of trust and cooperation with the communities they serve, emphasizing the importance of each interaction in shaping public perception.

As previously mentioned, the tragic death of George Floyd marked another pivotal point in the public consciousness regarding police use of force, particularly in the context of racial disparities. It revealed an urgent need for police reform and highlighted the critical role of public trust in effective law enforcement.

The widespread protests, riots, and calls for justice that followed were fueled by a deep-seated perception of systemic injustice within law enforce-ment agencies.

The video footage of Chauvin kneeling on Floyd's upper back for over nine minutes while Floyd repeatedly said, "*I can't breathe*," confirmed the belief by many that Black people suffer from police brutality far too often.

This perception was not limited to a singular event but was indicative of a history of strained relationships between law enforcement and, partic-ularly, communities of color. The statistics from the Pew Research Center survey further show the depth of this trust deficit and the perception of unequal treatment that persists in America.

According to a Pew Research Center survey conducted in June 2020, 67 percent of Americans said they felt police do not treat racial and ethnic groups equally, and 69 percent believed that the death of Floyd was a sign of a broader problem in law enforcement. The same survey also found that 58 percent of Black adults said they did not have confidence in the police to treat them fairly.

Moreover, the fact that Floyd's death was recorded and disseminated across social media platforms showed the power of modern technology to instantly and powerfully broadcast incidents of police conduct to a global audience. Such visuals profoundly impact public opinion and underscore the need for law enforcement to adopt measures that ensure accountability and justice.

Of course, the condemnation of the officers' actions by all the major professional law enforcement organizations, such as the IACP, PERF, NOBLE, and others, as well as police chiefs across the United States, was an important acknowledgment of the severity of the incident and highlighted the gap between professional standards and individual actions.

In the wake of these events, many police departments have revisited their community engagement strategies, use-of-force policies, and overall approach to law enforcement. These initiatives are steps in the right direction, aiming to rebuild trust, ensure fairness, and protect citizens' rights. However, building trust is a long-term endeavor that requires consistency, transparency, and a genuine commitment to change from law enforcement agencies.

The balance that law enforcement must strike is between the necessary use of force to protect public safety and the imperative to maintain the public's willing cooperation. Without voluntary public support, the fundamental principle of policing by consent, as envisioned by Sir Robert Peel, is undermined.

The evolution of public sentiment and legal scrutiny in the aftermath of the death of George Floyd has led to a growing call for a reassessment of the established standards of Graham v. Connor governing police use of force.

The heart of this shift lies in the concept of "*officer-created jeopardy*," a framework that scrutinizes the actions leading up to the necessity to use force. This approach suggests that an officer's prior conduct may unjustly precipitate a situation where force becomes necessary, which could otherwise have been avoided.

Courts of Appeals and other judicial bodies have started to examine use-of-force incidents through this lens, raising questions about the adequacy of current standards and training. By considering whether an officer's decisions or actions unnecessarily escalated a situation to the point where force was employed, a more nuanced understanding of "*reasonable force*" emerges.[40]

---

40   "2017 Supreme Court Case of County of Los Angeles v. Mendez," Legal Liability Risk Management Institute, accessed June 3, 2023, https://www.llrmi.com/articles/legal_update/2017_supreme_court_mendez/.

This judicial trend stresses the need for law enforcement training to not only cover the moment force is used but also to emphasize the importance of de-escalation techniques, decision-making under stress, and tactical repositioning to prevent violent encounters from occurring in the first place.

The legislative shifts in police use of force policies, particularly in states like California, signify a significant realignment in law enforcement protocol. The transition from a *"reasonable"* to a *"necessary"* standard for applying force represents a substantial elevation in the threshold that officers must meet before engaging in physical or deadly force.[41]

The policy shift within the Camden County Police Department to limit the use of force to a *"last resort"* is emblematic of a progressive approach to policing that prioritizes de-escalation and preserving life. This policy change is a response to a growing demand for law enforcement strategies that reduce the potential for force and conflict during police interactions with the community.[42]

This change is reflective of a broader societal call for police reform, emphasizing the sanctity of life and the minimization of violent encounters between law enforcement and the public. Under the necessary standard, the use of force is justified only when there is no reasonable alternative to resolve an incident safely. This compels officers to exhaust all other options before resorting to force, and when force is used, it must be proportional to the threat encountered.

While many changes are appropriate and necessary, there is a danger that some changes may make police officers less safe by causing them to hesitate too long before using force. The results of their hesitation could put their lives and the lives of others at risk.

In the contemporary law enforcement landscape, the strides made since Sir Robert Peel laid down his foundational principles are undeniable. Police officers in the current era are not only beneficiaries of

---

[41]   "California's new police use-of-force law is a 'significant' change," USA Today, accessed June 3, 2023, https://www.usatoday.com/story/news/nation/2019/08/20/california-new-police-use-force-law-significant-change/2068263001/.

[42]   "NJ police launch 'strict last resort' use-of-force policy," PoliceOne, accessed June 3, 2023, https://www.policeone.com/law-enforcement-policies/articles/nj-police-launch-strict-last-resort-use-of-force-policy-uHgrmit5mgTNWifn/.

sophisticated training and higher education but also embody a professional ethos that emphasizes restraint in applying force. Despite this progress, law enforcement is subject to unparalleled scrutiny, especially concerning the use of force.

To explain this transformation and combat misconceptions, it's instructive to examine compelling statistics highlighting the infrequency of force in police interactions. For instance, in 2020, amidst a staggering number of over 53.8 million police-citizen encounters, force was used only in a minute fraction of these engagements.[43] This data is a testament to the exceptional restraint and professionalism that characterize the modern-day police force and starkly contrast to the prevailing narratives of widespread aggressive policing.

The widespread use of social media, the proliferation of smartphones with video cameras, the use of body-worn cameras by law enforcement, and society's litigious nature have all contributed to the belief that excessive police use of force is a serious problem. Yet, the data suggests this is not accurate.

The nuanced complexities of police use of force extend far beyond the monochromatic portrayal often presented in public discourse. It envelops a spectrum of scenarios, from routine traffic enforcement to perilous engagements with armed adversaries. Each moment calls upon the officer to navigate a precarious terrain where decisions are forged in the crucible of urgency and uncertainty. Here, the dual imperatives of public guardianship and self-preservation coalesce, demanding a balance that is as delicate as it is imperative.

Consider, for instance, the typical police shooting. A look at the data reveals the presence of an armed suspect precipitates an overwhelming majority of such episodes. Despite the variances across jurisdictions in terms of reporting mechanisms and definitional boundaries, the thread of firearms' involvement weaves a consistent narrative through the tapestry of these violent confrontations.

This statistical revelation not only accentuates the dangerous waters that law enforcement must navigate but also brings to the forefront the

---

[43] Bureau of Justice Statistics (BJS), "Contacts Between Police and the Public, 2020," accessed May 31, 2023, https://bjs.ojp.gov/library/publications/contacts-between-police-and-public-2020.

contextual factors that must be integrated into any equitable evaluation of these incidents.

In a typical encounter, the officer, often facing an opaque situation, must discern intent, capability, and immediacy - the triad that governs the lawful application of lethal force. The officer must weigh the potential threat against the gravity of taking a life, all within the blink of an eye. Within this maelstrom of split-second decision-making, the officer's training, judgment, and adherence to protocol are put to the sternest of tests.

Statistical analyses and empirical data significantly influence the discourse on the use of force by police. For example, a meticulous examination by The Washington Post in 2019 revealed that out of an estimated annual tally of 1,000 fatal police shootings in the United States, a striking 90 percent or more involved individuals who were armed. This statistic paints a telling portrait of the conditions under which law enforcement officers often operate, highlighting the prevalence of a weapon as a common element in these most tragic outcomes.

Further bolstering this perspective is a 2018 publication in the Journal of Trauma and Acute Care Surgery, which identified the presence of firearms as a formidable predictor in the application of lethal force by police. Such data spotlights the fraught nature of the decisions facing officers in the field, where the delineation between life and death can hinge on the immediate assessment of potential threats.

These studies underline the somber realities of policing, a vocation where the potential for violent confrontation is an ever-present shadow. They recognize the importance of robust training and policies geared toward de-escalation and the judicious use of force.

The imperative for law enforcement to actively address both the reality and the public's perception of excessive force cannot be overstated. Proactivity is the key, not just in preventing occurrences of undue force but also in transforming public opinion on the frequency of such incidents. One potential avenue for achieving this is through educational initiatives that afford citizens a window into the split-second decision-making that defines many police encounters.

Firearms simulator training, a method extensively employed in law enforcement circles, immerses officers in varied scenarios that may necessitate the use of force. This form of training sharpens officers' decision-making skills by placing them in highly realistic, often stressful, shoot or don't shoot scenarios. By extending an invitation to citizens to participate in this form of training, law enforcement can offer a firsthand understanding of the complexities involved in such high-stakes situations.

A poignant example of the impact this training can have on public perception comes from Atlanta, where Reverend Markel Hutchins—a vocal civil rights advocate and occasional critic of police practices—was invited by the Atlanta Police Department to undergo firearms simulator training. His acceptance and subsequent experience within the simulation led to a transformative shift in his perspective.[44]

Although Reverend Hutchins maintained his commitment to civil rights advocacy, his firsthand experience provided him with a deeper appreciation for the nuanced challenges officers face in moments requiring a potential use of force. This insight galvanized his advocacy, shaping it into a form that recognized the value of working with law enforcement to instigate positive change.

Such collaborations between law enforcement and community leaders can serve as a powerful conduit for understanding and progress. They can help to demystify the split-second judgments officers must make and foster a dialogue that is informed by the realities of policing. It is these forms of engagement that can help bridge divides, nurture trust, and lead to the implementation of effective, community-supported policing strategies.

The responsibility of law enforcement extends far beyond the mere application of force; it encompasses the establishment of robust policies that dictate when and how force should be utilized. Such policies are the bedrock of accountability and are crucial in guiding officers through the maze of high-pressure situations. Yet, policies alone are not sufficient. Rigorous and ongoing training is essential to ensure that these policies are deeply ingrained in officers' practical, day-to-day actions. This training must cover the mechanics of force and the legal and ethical frameworks surrounding its use.

Each incident involving police use of force necessitates a meticulous review process. These reviews help identify deviations from established

---

[44] Atlanta Journal-Constitution, "Civil Rights Activist Participates in Police Shooting Simulation," accessed May 31, 2023, https://www.ajc.com/news/national/civil-rights-activist-participates-police-shooting-simulation/cZVf5MxtjqTs3 AnVyM7I3J/.

procedures, provide opportunities for learning and improvement, and, when necessary, initiate corrective actions. They serve as a critical feedback loop, enhancing officers' decision-making skills and reinforcing the standards to which they must adhere.

What is counted as a police use of force may vary from department to department. For example, the Dunwoody Police Department counts the drawing of a taser pointed at someone but not deploying the taser as a use of force. This is not the case in some departments.

In every instance where the use of deadly force is exercised by police officers, it is imperative that an independent criminal investigation be conducted by an external agency. This investigation should be thorough, unbiased, and detached from any local law enforcement influence to ensure its integrity. Upon completion, a comprehensive report detailing the findings of this investigation must be promptly submitted to the district attorney's office. This process is crucial to maintain public trust and ensure that each case involving the use of deadly force is subjected to an appropriate level of scrutiny.

Moreover, the tenor of each police encounter can significantly influence public perceptions and cooperation. Officers who engage with the public in a fair and respectful manner foster an environment of mutual trust and respect. Such interactions can lead to a community that is more willing to cooperate with law enforcement, which, in turn, can enhance the effectiveness of policing efforts.

Law enforcement agencies must proactively work towards gaining the public's willing cooperation. This task cannot be accomplished by force or intimidation; instead, it requires a consistent demonstration of professionalism, fairness, and respect in every community interaction. When the public perceives that law enforcement is acting in their best interests and with due regard for their rights and dignity, the foundation for cooperative police-community relations is laid.

Peel's Principles in Practice: Questions for Today's Challenges and Opportunities

Police Officers

1. What specific training programs are in place to ensure members of your department apply force judiciously and proportionately?
2. In what ways are officers encouraged to engage with the community to build trust and cooperation?
3. What mechanisms exist for officers to report and address misconduct within your ranks?
4. How does your department's recruitment and training reflect the diversity of the community you serve?
5. What are the procedures for independent review of incidents where force is used, and how does the department ensure transparency and accountability?
6. How is technology, such as body-worn cameras, integrated into the department's operations to enhance accountability and public trust?
7. Does your police department have access to firearms simulator training?
8. How much of your police department budget is devoted to training? One percent is a good starting place.
9. Does your police department provide scenario-based desescalation training?

Citizens

1. How does your police department ensure officers' use of force is thoroughly reviewed?
2. How accessible and transparent are your department's policies and procedures to the public?
3. What kind of civilian oversight exists, and how can civilians participate in or influence police conduct?
4. How does your police department foster relationships with community leaders and activists to address concerns of policing and civil rights?
5. In what ways does your department prioritize de-escalation and conflict resolution in their interactions with the community?
6. How does your department engage with the public to educate them about the complexities and challenges of police work?
7. Do the demographics of your local police department reflect the demographics of the community they serve?
8. Does your local police department have a Civilian Review Board or a Civilian Advisory Board?
9. Does your local police department have a program where citizens can experience scenario-based firearms simulator training?

PRINCIPLE #5

*To seek and preserve public favor, not by **pandering** to public opinion, but by constantly demonstrating absolute **impartial** service to the law, in complete independence of policy, and without regard to the justice or injustice of the substance of individual laws, by the ready offering of individual **service** and **friendship** to all members of the public, without regard to their wealth or social standing, by the ready exercise of **courtesy** and **friendly** good humor, and by the willing offering of individual **sacrifice** in protecting and preserving life.*

This principle speaks to the essence of policing by consent, a concept that is foundational to democratic societies. It underscores the notion that police legitimacy arises not from the power of the force but from the fair and equitable application of the law. This fairness and impartiality garner public favor—not as a popularity contest but as a reflection of the community's trust and confidence in its police force.

In the contemporary context, seeking public favor is not about courting public opinion but about earning public trust through consistent, just, and accountable actions. This includes an unwavering commitment to impartiality and fairness, where actions are not swayed by public sentiment but are grounded in legal and ethical policing standards.

Police officers are expected to embody the law, acting without prejudice or preference. This impartial service is not merely a procedural adherence but a demonstration of the values that underpin justice. In this light, departments across the nation are tasked with developing comprehensive policies that articulate these values and establish clear expectations for officer conduct. The accompanying training must address the complex layers of implicit bias and cultural competency, ensuring officers can engage with diverse communities knowledgeably and respectfully.

Moreover, Sir Robert Peel's caution against pandering is particularly relevant in an era where the immediacy of social media can amplify public opinion. Law enforcement agencies must navigate these waters carefully, ensuring that their actions are not reactive to public opinion but are proactive in upholding the principles of justice and due process. Policymaking and enforcement must be guided by the rule of law and ethical considerations, not by the fluctuating currents of public favor.

The symbol of Lady Justice is one we are all familiar with. In many early depictions, she had her eyes closed. But, since the 16th century, Lady Justice has worn a blindfold.[45]

The blindfold on Lady Justice represents the principle of objectivity, implying that justice should be dispensed without fear or favor, regardless of identity, money, power, or weakness. This iconic symbol serves as a poignant reminder to law enforcement that they must serve justice in a manner that is not influenced by external perceptions or internal prejudices.

The blindfold also signifies that justice is not swayed by the visual appearance of a defendant or victim, ensuring that all are equal before the law. In modern policing, this symbolism translates into a commitment to equity and fairness. Police officers must conduct their duties with a metaphorical blindfold, ensuring that their actions are not colored by the race, status, or background of the individuals they encounter.

Blind justice is integral to the rule of law in democratic societies. It's an ideal that police officers strive to achieve, understanding that the

---

[45] "Lady Justice," Wikipedia, accessed June 3, 2023, https://en.wikipedia.org/wiki/Lady_Justice#:~:text=Lady%20Justice%20(Latin%3A%20Iustitia),a%20mirror%20and%20a%20snake.

legitimacy of their authority is derived from their ability to apply the law equitably. Officers must be vigilant against allowing personal biases to influence their judgment, as even the perception of partiality can erode public trust.

For law enforcement, the blindfold of Lady Justice can also represent the impartial gathering of facts before making a judgment. It is a visual warning that police officers must gather evidence and ascertain facts without prejudice, allowing the truth to guide their actions rather than preconceived notions or societal pressures.

Lady Justice holds the scales of justice in one hand and wields a sword in the other.

The embodiment of Lady Justice carrying scales and a sword is a powerful symbol in the administration of law and justice. Delicately balanced scales are emblematic of law enforcement's duty to weigh the evidence with meticulous care and impartiality. This image impresses upon officers the importance of thorough investigation and consideration of all relevant factors before acting.

The sword she holds is not just a symbol of power but of the precision and decisiveness required of the justice system. It reminds law enforcement that their actions have significant consequences and must be wielded judiciously and proportionately. The sword represents the enforcement arm of the law, affirming that while justice must be delivered fairly, it must also be resolute and capable of protecting society from harm.

When integrated into the context of modern law enforcement, these symbols instruct officers to balance evidence and enforce the law impartially, ensuring that justice is neither arbitrary nor capricious. It also serves as a visual representation of the dual responsibilities of police officers: to protect the community while respecting the rights of individuals.

Respecting the rights of others leads to police legitimacy, which is foundational to maintaining public trust and ensuring the effectiveness of law enforcement within a community. When police officers embody the principles of impartiality and fairness, they strengthen the public's perception of the police as a legitimate authority.

Police legitimacy is not merely about the lawful exercise of power; it is also about perceived justice in the eyes of the public. It encompasses the belief that the police act in ways consistent with the community's sense of right and wrong. This perception is crucial, as it directly influences the willingness of community members to obey laws, cooperate with police directives, and contribute to maintaining public order.[46]

To foster police legitimacy, departments must commit to transparency and accountability. Officers should be trained to engage with the community proactively, emphasizing the importance of communication, understanding, and respect for individual rights. Furthermore, departments should establish mechanisms to address grievances and misconduct, demonstrating a commitment to justice in the streets and within their ranks.

The principle of absolute impartial service to the law anchors itself in the foundational duty of police officers to enforce laws equitably, without personal judgment clouding their responsibilities. Sir Robert Peel's emphasis on this impartiality aimed to establish a policing system free from political biases, ensuring that law enforcement was not swayed by social status or political connections.

When Peel wrote these principles in 1829, there was little diversity in London as we know it today. People were divided by class, rich or poor, politically connected or not. When Peel spoke about absolute impartial service to the law without regard to the law's justice or injustice, the comment must be taken in context. Peel was trying to develop a professional law enforcement agency without political influence.

Furthermore, the principle of absolute impartial service to the law requires police officers to be independent of policy and without regard to the justice or injustice of individual laws. It is not the role of the police to decide which laws are just or unjust. Their job is to enforce the law impartially, without fear or favor.

In law enforcement, the tension between personal convictions and professional obligations is an ongoing challenge. Police officers are tasked with upholding laws that, while legally binding, may not always align with their moral compass or societal expectations of justice. This dichotomy underscores the importance of ethical frameworks within police departments, which guide officers on how to uphold the law while maintaining their integrity and public trust.

These ethical frameworks are vital, especially when officers encounter laws that may be antiquated or perceived as unjust. It is in these moments

46   "Police legitimacy," Wikipedia, accessed June 3, 2023, https://en.wikipedia.org/wiki/Police_legitimacy.

that the principle of discretion comes into play. Discretion allows officers to assess each situation and determine the most appropriate course of action, which may involve measures other than strict enforcement.

Discretion, however, is not an avenue for arbitrary decision-making; it is a responsibility exercised within the bounds of legal standards and departmental policy. It requires a nuanced understanding of the community's needs and the potential impact of an officer's actions.[47]

The multifaceted role of a police officer requires not only adherence to laws and regulations but also the wisdom to interpret and apply them with discernment. The concept of discretion is intrinsic to policing, providing officers the latitude to navigate the myriad situations they encounter daily. A commitment to the principles of justice and public welfare governs the exercise of discretion.

For instance, in scenarios where legal directives are clear and consequential, such as instances of violent crime, an officer's discretion is naturally circumscribed by the gravity of the offense. In these cases, the law dictates a clear path that officers must follow, leaving little room for personal judgment.

On the other end of the spectrum, there are instances where the law allows for flexibility, enabling officers to make choices that may favor rehabilitation over punishment, such as in the case of public intoxication. Here, the officer may decide that the individual's safety and public order are best served by alternatives to arrest, such as safe transportation to the individual's home. Such decisions address the immediate concern and reflect a compassionate approach that may prevent further incidents.

Moreover, discretion is essential when laws do not adequately reflect the complexities of real-life situations. It acts as a buffer, allowing officers to interpret the spirit of the law rather than adhere rigidly to the letter, especially in cases that involve minor infractions or where the application of the law may result in more significant harm than the offense itself.

Furthermore, discretion supports proactive policing by empowering officers to resolve problems before they escalate. In applying discretion,

47   "Police Discretion - Definition," Encyclopedia.com, accessed June 3, 2023, https://www.encyclopedia.com/articles/police-discretion-definition/#:~:text=Discretion%20means%20the%20power%20and,the%20people%20they%20are%20policing.

officers can take preventive measures, such as mediating disputes or issuing warnings, thereby defusing potential conflicts, and reducing the likelihood of future infractions.

However, with the power of discretion comes the need for accountability. Officers must be prepared to justify their decisions and actions, particularly when they deviate from standard procedures. Transparency in discretion is paramount to maintaining public trust and ensuring that decisions are made in the interest of justice and community safety.

Ultimately, the judicious use of discretion is a hallmark of effective policing, allowing officers to act as guardians of public safety while respecting the rights and dignity of individuals. The nuanced application of discretion, informed by law, ethics, and community values, enables police officers to navigate the complexities of their role and serve the public with integrity and fairness.

In 1999, the National Institute of Justice (NIJ) produced a research report titled Broken Windows and Police Discretion.[48] The NIJ document is an exhaustive report about police discretion and is worth reading.

The report produced by the session underscored the role of discretion in handling minor offenses like disorderly conduct and advocating for its use to de-escalate potential conflicts. This approach promotes a more humane and effective policing model, recognizing that rigid enforcement in every instance can be counterproductive and exacerbate tensions within communities.

However, the effective implementation of discretion comes with its challenges. Officers often operate under the eye of various stakeholders, from supervisors and peers to the communities they serve. These external pressures can impinge their ability to exercise judgment freely, sometimes compelling them to act in ways that may not align with the ethos of discretion.

To safeguard against the improper use of discretion, law enforcement agencies are encouraged to establish explicit policies that clearly define acceptable practices. These policies should resolutely prohibit racial profiling and any form of bias-based policing, integrate the principles of

---

[48]   "Understanding and Improving Police Use of Force," National Criminal Justice Reference Service, accessed June 3, 2023, https://www.ncjrs.gov/pdffiles1/nij/178259.pdf.

procedural justice, and provide clear guidelines on the permissible scope of officer discretion.

The NIJ document recognized that while discretion is a tool for more personalized and community-oriented policing, it must be grounded in a framework that ensures fairness, transparency, and accountability. To this end, standard operating procedures serve as a blueprint, guiding officers in the ethical exercise of discretion while ensuring that their actions are in harmony with the values of justice and equality that underpin the mission of law enforcement.

The dialogue around police discretion continues to evolve, reflecting the dynamic interplay between the principles of justice and the practical realities of policing. As law enforcement agencies strive to enhance their service to the public, the conscientious deployment of discretion remains a cornerstone of their efforts to maintain public safety, uphold the law, and foster trust within their communities.

In 2013, the Bureau of Justice Assistance (BJA) conducted an Executive Session on Police Leadership. They assembled a multi-discipline panel to discuss many important issues. One of the topics addressed was police discretion.[49]

There were eight videos in this series. This discussion will focus on video #2, Rethinking Peel's Principle #5: The Case for Discretion in Modern Policing.

Professor Michael Scott, a former police chief, shared a story about when he was appointed police chief. He wanted a policy about police discretion, but he couldn't find one when he checked with multiple other agencies. Instead of being discouraged, Chief Scott wrote a policy.

In this video, the panelists discussed the importance of using discretion appropriately and being held accountable for that use of discretion. They even discussed how police discretion diminishes as the issue becomes more serious.

Peel's principles regarding the absolute impartial service of law enforcement officers to the law remain as pertinent today as in the 19th century, if not more so in our contemporary, highly diverse, and scrutinized society. This principle serves as a foundation for the expectations and

---

[49] "Rethinking Sir Robert Peel's Nine Principles," BJA Leadership Institute, accessed June 3, 2023, http://bjaleader.org/pdfs/010.2RethinkingPeel5.pdf.

responsibilities of police officers to serve every member of the community fairly and without prejudice.

Offering friendship and individual service to all members of the public is a cornerstone of community policing. It emphasizes the importance of police officers being accessible and approachable to people from all walks of life, ensuring that no preference is shown due to a person's social or economic status. This approach builds trust and fosters a cooperative relationship between the police and the community they serve.

The second aspect, which calls for courteous treatment and friendly, good humor, recognizes the power of approachability and relatability in law enforcement. An officer's ability to interact with the public in a respectful and personable manner can defuse tensions and contribute to more positive outcomes in policing situations. Humor, when used judiciously, can be a bridge between law enforcement and the community, humanizing officers and breaking down barriers.

For example, many law enforcement agencies use humor exceedingly well on their social media channels. Humor helps these departments better connect with the community.

The third element of Peel's guidance—the willingness to sacrifice—is a testament to the dedication that law enforcement officers must possess. This selfless commitment to protecting the community is a fundamental aspect of the profession, often requiring officers to face dangerous situations to ensure public safety. This very essence of bravery and self-sacrifice garners respect and establishes the legitimacy of the police force in the eyes of the community.

In addressing the need for impartial enforcement of the law, training and support are essential for officers to perform their duties effectively. Providing ongoing education in areas such as cultural competency, de-escalation techniques, and ethical policing practices is vital in preparing officers for the diverse challenges they face.

As society evolves, so too does the context within which policing occurs. The principles of Sir Robert Peel stand as enduring reminders of the values that should guide law enforcement: fairness, respect, and a commitment to service above self.

By embodying these values, police officers can navigate the complexities of modern policing while maintaining the trust and confidence of those they have sworn to protect and serve. But if police officers fail in this endeavor, bad outcomes are inevitable.

The widespread protests after the death of George Floyd, combined with calls for police reform, sent a message to law enforcement that there needs to be changes in how the community is policed. The 2020 Gallup Poll on police trust shows trust in the police declined after the death of George Floyd, especially for minorities.[50]

As law enforcement moves forward, police officers must work harder to build positive relationships with those they serve, especially those in minority communities. They also must be willing to institute police reforms where it makes sense.

By following this principle, police officers can build trust with members of the public, reduce crime and disorder, and help maintain law and order in our communities.

---

[50] "Americans' confidence in police falls to new low, Gallup poll shows," USA Today, accessed June 3, 2023, https://www.usatoday.com/story/news/nation/2020/08/12/americans-confidence-police-falls-new-low-gallup-poll-shows/3352910001/.

Peel's Principles in Practice: Questions for Today's Challenges and Opportunities

Police Officers

1. How does your department define and measure police legitimacy?
2. Does your police department have a bias-based policing policy?
3. Do supervisors at your police department ever engage in conversations about treating people fairly and impartially?
4. What steps are taken to maintain professional discretion while preventing arbitrary decision-making?
5. What mechanisms are in place for the public to report grievances and misconduct?
6. How does your department balance the need for enforcement with the community's sense of justice?

Citizens

1. How does your police department ensure fair and equitable application of the law?
2. What are your police department's policies on police discretion, and how are they implemented?
3. In what ways can citizens contribute to or participate in your department's policy-making process?
4. How does your department address community grievances and incidents of police misconduct?

5. How transparent is your department about its actions and decisions?
6. How has your department responded to the calls for police reform, especially considering recent events and public opinion polls?
7. What have your interactions with your local police department been like?

PRINCIPLE #6

*To use physical force **only** when the exercise of **persuasion**, **advice**, and **warning** is found to be insufficient to obtain public co-operation to an extent necessary to secure observance of the law or to restore order, and to use only the **minimum** degree of physical force which is necessary on any particular occasion for achieving a police objective.*

The language surrounding law enforcement's use of force profoundly impacts the public's perception of its legitimacy. While the term *"police violence"* is commonly used in some circles to describe instances of force by law enforcement, it is essential to differentiate between violence and the application of force within the bounds of the law and departmental policies.

Police violence implies an unlawful or illegitimate use of force with an intent to harm, which can unjustly conflate all uses of force with misconduct or abuse.[51] On the other hand, law enforcement's use of physical force, when applied correctly, is a sanctioned aspect of policing that is subject to strict regulations and oversight. This force is employed to protect

---

51   Police Violence Report, accessed May 31, 2023, https://policeviolencereport.org/.

the public and the officers themselves, often in circumstances that are volatile and fraught with immediate danger.

Some citizens view law enforcement's use of force as something done to them, while law enforcement views police use of force as a necessary part of their duties.

Some websites and databases track instances of force used by police, which can serve as valuable resources for analysis, transparency, and accountability. While necessary for oversight, these tools can sometimes contribute to a narrative that does not fully capture the complexity of police work or the context within which force is used.

It is incumbent upon law enforcement agencies and the community to engage in open, honest dialogues about police use of force. These discussions should be grounded in facts and understanding the legal and procedural frameworks governing police action. Education and awareness initiatives can help demystify law enforcement's use of force, clarifying the distinction between necessary, legally justified force and illegitimate violence.

Furthermore, agencies must ensure that their officers are equipped with the necessary training, including de-escalation techniques, to minimize the need for force. This training, combined with the use of body-worn cameras and community policing strategies, can help to build trust between law enforcement and the communities they serve.

The historical perspective on law enforcement's use of force reveals a significant evolution in practices and public perception. In the mid-19th century, when formal police departments were establishing their roots in the United States, there was a distinct lack of nationwide coordination, unlike the centralized model found in England. American officers were confined to their municipal jurisdictions, often hindering efforts to combat crime effectively.

During this period, the use of force by police was seen as a primary means to control and deter criminal activity. This led to the emergence of the archetypal *"tough street cop,"* a figure who ostensibly maintained order through physical coercion and punitive measures.[52] Such an

---

[52] "English and American policing in the late 19th century," Britannica, accessed June 3, 2023, https://www.britannica.com/topic/police/English-and-American-policing-in-the-late-19th-century.

approach to policing was not only a response to the practical limitations of the time but also reflective of the broader societal attitudes towards crime and punishment.

In the late 1800s, politicians used the police to exert political control, especially with immigrant populations.[53]

However, this reliance on physical force as a primary law enforcement tool was eventually scrutinized more closely. As society's understanding of human rights evolved and the principles of justice and due process became more deeply ingrained in the fabric of American democracy, the role of physical force in policing was reexamined.

Today, while there is recognition that force is sometimes necessary to ensure public safety and officer protection, there is also a consensus that it should be used sparingly and judiciously. Modern policing strategies emphasize the importance of de-escalation, communication, and community engagement to prevent crime and manage incidents. The use of force is increasingly seen as a last resort rather than a first response.

Moreover, there is an acute awareness of the disparate impact that the use of force can have on minority communities. This has led to calls for reform and a reevaluation of how force is applied to ensure that law enforcement treats all individuals, regardless of background, equally. Efforts to address these concerns include the implementation of bias training, the promotion of diversity within police forces, and the adoption of body cameras to provide transparency and accountability.

Reflecting on the past, it's clear that the ethos of policing in America has undergone profound changes. The journey from the tough street cop to the community-focused officer of today illustrates a broader shift towards more compassionate, community-centric, and rights-respecting law enforcement practices. As society continues to evolve, so too will the philosophies and tactics that underpin the critical work of police officers.

The historical landscape of American law enforcement is marred by episodes where the application of force was inextricably linked with oppressive legal systems and discriminatory practices. Under the guise of maintaining order and enforcing the law, various institutions, including the police and, at times, even the military, were complicit in upholding the Jim Crow laws that enforced racial segregation. These laws, spanning from

---

[53] ibid

the post-Reconstruction era until the mid-20th century, institutionalized a system of subjugation and disenfranchisement for African Americans.[54]

Moreover, the forceful displacement of Native Americans from their ancestral lands, executed under the authority of government policies, represents another dark chapter wherein law enforcement, along with the military, played a pivotal role. The systematic suppression and marginalization of indigenous populations, often through violent means, laid the foundation for centuries of conflict and injustice that have had lasting repercussions.

These historical instances reflect a broader pattern of the use of force to suppress and control various minority and marginalized groups across the country. Using force in these contexts was not merely about upholding the law; it was a tool for enforcing a social order based on racial and cultural hierarchies.

In contemporary society, the legacy of these actions continues to influence public perceptions of policing and the justice system. The critical reassessment of past practices has sparked a movement to ensure that law enforcement agencies serve all segments of society equitably and humanely. This includes acknowledging historical injustices, reforming practices that may disproportionately affect certain groups, and engaging in reconciliation and community building.

Today's policing efforts are increasingly focused on fostering trust and cooperation within communities, using force only when necessary and within the bounds of strict ethical and legal standards. There is a growing emphasis on community-oriented policing, cultural competency, and the protection of civil rights, with the goal of not repeating past mistakes. This shift reflects the ongoing endeavor to align law enforcement practices with the principles of justice, equality, and respect for human dignity.

---

54   "The Invention of the Police," The New Yorker, accessed June 3, 2023, https://www.newyorker.com/magazine/2020/07/20/the-invention-of-the-police?irclickid=0fq0L6TKoxyOT3EwUx0Mo3YQUkEya3wRyQZvxk0&irgwc=1&source=affiliate_impactpmx_12f6tote_desktop_adgoal%20GmbH&utm_source=impact-affiliate&utm_medium=123201&utm_campaign=impact&utm_content=Online%20Tracking%20Link&utm_brand=tny.

In 1963, Martin Luther King delivered his I Have a Dream speech. As part of this speech, King said, *"We can never be satisfied as long as the Negro is the victim of unspeakable horrors of police brutality."*[55]

The sentiment expressed by Martin Luther King and the evolution of policing techniques, particularly regarding the use of force, reflects the law enforcement community's commitment to progress and reform. Modern police officers benefit from advanced training, a comprehensive understanding of the legal landscape, and various non-lethal tools designed to resolve conflicts with minimal harm. These developments underscore the significant shift from past practices and a dedication to lawful and ethical engagement with the communities they serve.

Despite these advances, the journey towards perfecting the application of force in policing is ongoing. Acknowledging this, law enforcement leaders have taken steps to implement change and address historical wrongs. A pivotal moment in this journey came in 2016 when Terry Cunningham, then President of the International Association of Chiefs of Police (IACP), extended an official apology for the historical mistreatment of communities of color. This unprecedented gesture of repentance, made during the annual IACP banquet, symbolized a recognition of the need for healing and the importance of building bridges with those who have borne the brunt of past injustices.[56]

Terry Cunningham's public apology at the 2016 IACP banquet was a pivotal moment in policing history, signifying a commitment to reckon with and address past injustices perpetrated under the guise of law enforcement. This act of contrition, reflective of a broader call for accountability, recognizes the complexities and the often painful legacy within marginalized communities.

---

[55] "How Police Fought Civil Rights Reform—And Lost," Time, accessed June 3, 2023, https://time.com/5882308/march-on-washington-police-brutality/.

[56] "Head of Police Chiefs Group Apologizes for 'Historical Mistreatment' of Minorities," NPR, accessed June 3, 2023, https://www.npr.org/sections/thetwo-way/2016/10/18/498380373/head-of-police-chiefs-group-apologizes-for-historical-mistreatment-of-minorities#:~:text=Press-,Head%20Of%20Police%20Chiefs%20Group%20Apologizes%20For%20'Historical%20Mistreatment'%20Of,Association%20of%20Chiefs%20of%20Police.

The impact of such an apology lies in its potential to foster healing and pave the way for rebuilding trust between law enforcement and the public. It signals a readiness to change and progress beyond dated and discriminatory practices. Such public acknowledgments are integral to community reconciliation and the development of equitable policing strategies.

Moreover, this gesture underscores the responsibility of law enforcement agencies to reflect critically on their roles and responsibilities. It encourages a necessary shift from defensive posturing to proactive engagement and reform. The apology is not the end goal but rather a significant step in an ongoing journey toward a more just and empathetic approach to policing.

In the context of Cunningham's apology and the ensuing dialogue, law enforcement's mission remains straightforward: to protect and serve with honor, recognize the sanctity of all lives, and commit to democracy and human dignity. The path forward requires continued effort and collaboration with community stakeholders to ensure that policing practices reflect the values of the society they serve.

Such acknowledgments and tangible reforms represent key strides in reshaping the relationship between police and the diverse populations they serve. The IACP's apology reflects a broader law enforcement initiative to reconcile with past practices and forge a future where the use of force by police is not only legally justified but also morally and socially responsible.

In this vein, police departments focus on continuous improvement in areas such as de-escalation techniques, crisis intervention, and community engagement. They are also increasingly transparent, holding officers accountable through measures like body-worn cameras and independent oversight.

In this context of transformation and accountability, law enforcement continues to refine its approach to using force, striving to balance the imperative of public safety with the rights and dignity of individuals. The goal is a policing model that not only protects but also preserves the community's trust, ensuring that every use of force is justified, proportionate, and in line with the community's values and expectations.

Policing, as a dynamic profession, continuously evolves its practices and approaches to uphold public safety while ensuring the rights and dignity of individuals are respected. The core idea of this principle of using the minimum degree of physical force necessary reflects the commitment to proportional response—a fundamental aspect of modern law enforcement.

This principle demands that officers assess each situation individually and choose a course of action that is necessary and reasonable under the circumstances. It's not just about the application of force but its judicious and ethical application, aligning actions closely with the seriousness of the offense and the immediate threat to officer or public safety.

Adopting de-escalation tactics represents a shift towards communication and crisis intervention skills in policing. These tactics reduce tension, facilitate voluntary compliance, and avoid force whenever possible. De-escalation training is integrated into the curriculum of police academies and in-service programs, highlighting its importance in contemporary policing.

Moreover, embracing less-lethal technology and methods is part of this commitment to minimizing harm. Tools such as tasers, pepper spray, and bean bag rounds, when used correctly, can subdue a threat without resorting to lethal force.

There have been tremendous advancements in recent years around de-escalation, which is really what this principle is addressing. By exercising persuasion, advice, and warning, Peel suggested that police officers do everything possible to avoid using force.

Although the word de-escalation hadn't been invented yet, the early idea of the concept was developed in 1829.

Conflict resolution and de-escalation techniques have become critical components of modern police training. Officers are trained to manage high-pressure situations by actively listening, showing empathy, and employing effective communication strategies. By utilizing these skills, officers can defuse potentially volatile encounters, reduce tension, and minimize the need for physical force.

In recent years, de-escalation training has been implemented in agencies across the country and is sometimes viewed by the public as the solution to police use of force. However, even when police officers use de-escalation techniques properly, there could still be a use of force, including deadly force.

In 2018, the Governor of Georgia mandated four hours of de-escalation training every year for all peace officers in Georgia. A similar requirement for de-escalation training has also been implemented in other states.[57]

---

[57] Georgia Public Safety Training Center (GPSTC), "GPSTC Answers Governor's Call," accessed May 31, 2023, https://www.gpstc.org/featured-training/gpstc-answers-governors-call/.

One of the most outstanding de-escalation training examples is the Integrating Communications, Assessment, and Tactics (ICAT) training developed by the Police Executive Research Forum (PERF).

ICAT is designed to equip police officers with the tools they need to safely defuse a wide range of critical incidents, especially situations involving unarmed people experiencing a mental health crisis.[58]

Creating time and distance to de-escalate encounters has helped improve the safety of police officers and citizens.

According to CBS News, a study by the Treatment Advocacy Center finds that approximately 25 percent of fatal encounters with law enforcement involve a person experiencing a mental health crisis.[59]

Other studies and reports have come to similar conclusions.

Fortunately, law enforcement today has tools, in addition to de-escalation training, to help them interact better with those experiencing a mental health crisis.

Crisis Intervention Team training has been delivered to thousands of police officers nationwide. This 40-hour training class has been widely implemented and accepted and is a great resource for law enforcement.

One study found that CIT-trained officers could negotiate better, were less likely to arrest people, and were more likely to make a mental health referral than officers who were not CIT-trained.[60]

The IACP, in partnership with the Bureau of Justice Assistance, developed the One-Mind Campaign and Pledge, which seeks to ensure interactions between law enforcement and people experiencing mental health issues have a positive outcome.[61]

---

58   "ICAT Training Guide," Police Executive Research Forum, accessed June 3, 2023, https://www.policeforum.org/icat-training-guide.

59   "How Mental Illness Affects Police Shooting Fatalities," International Bipolar Foundation, accessed June 3, 2023, https://ibpf.org/how-mental-illness-affects-police-shooting-fatalities/.

60   "Gun Violence Restraining Orders: A Promising Strategy to Reduce Gun Violence," Journal of the American Academy of Psychiatry and the Law Online, accessed June 3, 2023, http://jaapl.org/content/early/2019/09/24/JAAPL.003863-19.

61   "One Mind Campaign," International Association of Chiefs of Police, accessed June 3, 2023, https://www.theiacp.org/one-mind-pledge.

As part of the One Mind pledge, police departments agree to partner with a local community health organization, develop a policy related to mental health calls, and commit to training 20 percent of officers with Crisis Intervention Training and the remaining 80 percent with Mental Health First Aid training.[62]

In addition to the mental health challenges in communities, there has also been a lot of order disturbed since 2020. The riots that spread across the country after the death of George Floyd were unprecedented. Complicating the police response to these riots was the fact that the protests were directed at the police.

Therefore, police officers were in a challenging position. If they exercised proper control over the rioting groups, they could very well be accused of using excessive force. Conversely, they could be accused of not doing their job if they showed too much restraint.

Although many police departments found the right balance, others did not. For example, the oversight agency for the NYPD found that 92 police officers used excessive force during the many days of protest in the aftermath of the death of George Floyd in New York.[63] The chair of the Civilian Complaint Review Board, Arva Rice, wrote, "*Protests against police brutality bred more instances of police misconduct.*" This statement, sadly, appears to be true.

However, the statement does not consider the unprecedented number of protests police officers in New York and elsewhere faced. The level of violence and mix of criminal protesters intermingled with protesters exercising their constitutional rights made keeping order an even more significant challenge for the police. The added fact that many police officers were under-trained, under-equipped, lacked supervisory direction, and were outnumbered made the challenge even worse.

---

[62]   ibid

[63]   "Police Oversight Agency Finds Dozens of Officers Used Excessive Force in 2020 George Floyd Protests," NY1, accessed June 3, 2023, https://www.ny1.com/nyc/all-boroughs/news/2023/02/06/police-oversight-agency-finds-dozens-of-officers-used-excessive-force-in-2020-george-floyd-protests#:~:text=Police%20oversight%20agency%20finds%20dozens,in%202020%20George%20Floyd%20protests&text=The%20city's%20police%20oversight%20agency,George%20Floyd's%20death%20in%202020.

Protesters across the country also filed many lawsuits. For example, in Austin, Texas, officials agreed to pay $13 million to people injured in protests after the death of George Floyd. Also, 19 officers were indicted for their actions against protesters.[64] In December 2023, all charges were dropped against those officers.[65]

In Denver, a jury awarded 12 people who sued the City $14 million after finding that the Denver police used excessive force against protesters and violated their constitutional rights during the protests after the death of George Floyd.[66]

Police officers and the departments that employ them must do more to make sure officers are treating people fairly, constitutionally, and without using excessive force, even when faced with difficult circumstances, such as the protests and riots in the aftermath of the death of George Floyd.

There will likely be future protests and riots directed at the police. Therefore, the Boy Scout's motto of "*Be prepared*" is a critical mindset for departments to have in the future. Here are some suggestions on how the police can better prepare to handle protests and riots:

1. **Training and education**: Police officers must be trained and educated on handling protests and riots. They should be taught how to de-escalate tense situations, communicate effectively with protesters, and use nonviolent methods to control crowds. Officers should also be trained on the legal limits of their authority, the rights of protesters, and the consequences of excessive use of force.

---

[64] "19 Austin Police Officers Indicted from Investigation into 2020 Protests, Sources Say," NPR, accessed June 3, 2023, https://www.npr.org/2022/02/17/1081609073/19-austin-police-officers-indicted-from-investigation-into-2020-protests-sources.

[65] USA Today, "Use-of-force Charges Dropped for Austin Police in 2020 Protests," accessed May 31, 2023, https://www.usatoday.com/story/news/nation/2023/12/04/use-of-force-charges-dropped-austin-police-2020-protests/71805438007/.

[66] "Denver jury awards $14M to protesters who alleged police department used excessive force," CBS News, accessed June 3, 2023, https://www.cbsnews.com/news/george-floyd-denver-jury-awards-14m-to-protesters-who-alleged-police-department-used-excessive-force/.

2. **Planning and coordination**: Before a protest or rally, police should assess the potential risks and develop a comprehensive plan for handling the event. This includes identifying potential conflict areas, establishing clear communication lines with protesters and organizers, and ensuring adequate resources are available to respond to potential incidents.

3. **Communication and transparency**: Police should establish clear and effective communication with protesters, including providing them with information on the event's purpose, any restrictions or limitations on their activities, and any potential consequences for noncompliance. Police should also be transparent about their plans and actions, including using force, and be accountable for any misconduct.

4. **Use of force**: Police should use force only as a last resort and use the minimum amount necessary to control the situation. They should also be trained on the appropriate use of less-lethal weapons, such as tear gas and rubber bullets, and ensure that these weapons are only used in appropriate circumstances.

5. **Respect for human rights**: Police must respect the human rights of protesters, including their right to freedom of expression, assembly, and association. They should avoid any actions that may be perceived as discriminatory, such as targeting protesters based on their race, ethnicity, or political views.

6. **Prioritizing community policing**: Building positive relationships with communities can help police gain trust and cooperation during protests and rallies. Police departments should prioritize community policing efforts, including regular outreach and engagement with community leaders and residents. This can help establish a foundation of trust and understanding between police and communities, which can be essential during unrest.

7. **Using technology**: Technology can be a valuable tool for managing protests and riots. For example, police can use drones or other aerial surveillance to monitor crowd movements and identify potential risks. They can also use social media to communicate with protesters and the public, providing updates and instructions in real time.

8. **Establishing mutual aid agreements**: During large-scale protests or riots, police departments may need assistance from neighboring agencies. Establishing mutual aid agreements with other departments in advance can ensure that additional resources and personnel are available when needed.

9. **Reviewing and evaluating responses**: After a protest or riot, police departments should review their response, including any use of force or misconduct. They should also solicit feedback from protesters and the public to identify areas for improvement and implement changes accordingly. Regular evaluations can help police departments refine their strategies and better prepare for future events.

Handling protests and riots requires a multifaceted approach that prioritizes communication, de-escalation, and respect for human rights. By implementing these suggestions, police departments can better prepare to handle protests and rallies while promoting public safety and protecting individual rights.

Peel clarified that the police should only use force when all other alternatives have been exhausted.

Police officers today are fortunate. Unlike their counterparts in Peel's time, they have a variety of less-lethal options instead of resorting to physical force when they can't talk a person into cooperating.

Advancements in technology have provided law enforcement agencies with a range of non-lethal options. Tasers, pepper spray, rubber bullets, and other less-lethal weapons offer alternatives to deadly force while still enabling officers to protect themselves and others. These tools align with minimal force usage, allowing officers to respond appropriately to threats without resorting to lethal measures.

In the past, police officers documented their uses of force in their reports with the statement, *"Only the minimum force necessary was used to affect the arrest."* Little did most police officers realize that statement originated in one of Peel's principles.

Of course, that statement makes a lot of sense. Yet, it only tells part of the story. The action behind that statement tells the real story.

By consistently using the minimum force necessary when force must be used, police officers gain and maintain the trust and respect of the citizens they serve.

Today, completing a report by writing, "*Only the minimum force necessary was used to affect the arrest,*" is insufficient for police reports. Police officers must use language that precisely describes the actions of the suspect and the officer. For example, "*The suspect pushed me in the chest and turned to run. I reached out and grabbed the suspect by his left arm and pulled him to the ground.*"

Police use of force has been under extreme scrutiny of late, unlike at any point in history. George Floyd's death and the protests and riots that followed have caused law enforcement to examine their policies and search for solutions that will help them do their job better while protecting the public and maintaining trust with the community.

Law enforcement must accept the closer scrutiny of police use of force and acknowledge that they don't always get it right. Additionally, law enforcement must take proactive steps to reduce police use of force and ensure that force is only used in appropriate situations.

The public must also recognize the difficult job police officers have and take steps to reduce the chances of a bad outcome during a police encounter by cooperating with the police.

The notion of complete cooperation with law enforcement represents an aspirational benchmark, recognizing that, in practical terms, it may never be fully realized. However, the essence of this ideal highlights the pivotal role that mutual understanding, respect, and effective communication play in fostering safer interactions between police officers and the communities they serve.

Realistically, striving for substantial reductions in police use of force necessitates multifaceted approaches that address systemic issues, enhance police training and accountability, and foster community trust and engagement. By promoting transparency, accountability, and empathy within law enforcement agencies, alongside community outreach initiatives that prioritize dialogue and collaboration, opportunities emerge for meaningful progress in mitigating instances of excessive force.

Moreover, initiatives aimed at de-escalation techniques, cultural competency training, and mental health awareness among law enforcement personnel can significantly reduce the likelihood of forceful encounters. Recognizing the diverse factors influencing police-community interactions underscores the need for holistic strategies that encompass proactive measures aimed at prevention, intervention, and continuous improvement.

Ultimately, while achieving a 100 percent reduction in police use of force remains an aspirational goal, pursuing such an objective catalyzes ongoing dialogue, reform, and collaborative efforts aimed at cultivating safer communities for all. By prioritizing empathy, understanding, and mutual respect, stakeholders can collectively work towards realizing a future where unnecessary force is minimized and trust between law enforcement and the public is strengthened.

The National Organization of Black Law Enforcement Executives (NOBLE) has taken meaningful steps toward creating safer encounters between the police and the public through a training program titled The Law and Your Community.[67] This program has been taught nationally since 2014.

The American Civil Liberties Union speaks directly to this point about reducing the risk to citizens from a police encounter by suggesting that a person should stay calm, not run, resist, or obstruct officers, and not lie or give false documents.[68]

Ultimately, the more cooperation between the citizens and the police, the safer those encounters will be.

Sir Robert Peel's principle laid the groundwork for a policing philosophy that balances authority with civil liberties, emphasizing that using physical force should always be a last resort. He recognized that the power vested in law enforcement comes with a great responsibility—to protect without oppressing, to serve without violating trust. Peel's vision was to foster a force that upheld the law while earning the public's respect and cooperation, not one that instilled fear through unnecessary force.

---

[67] National Organization of Black Law Enforcement Executives (NOBLE), "The Law and Your Community," accessed May 31, 2023, https://noblenational.org/the-law-and-your-community/.

[68] American Civil Liberties Union (ACLU), "Stopped by Police," accessed May 31, 2023, https://www.aclu.org/know-your-rights/stopped-by-police/.

Peel's Principles in Practice: Questions for Today's Challenges and Opportunities

Police Officers

1. What specific de-escalation training programs does your department provide, and how often are officers required to complete them?

2. What policies does your department have that define the appropriate use of force, and how does the department ensure that all officers understand these policies?

3. Has your police department signed on to the IACP One Mind campaign?

4. How is your department preparing for potential future protests or riots, and what protocols are in place to balance control with respect for citizens' rights?

5. Does your department conduct after-action reviews of its response to protests or riots?

6. What partnerships or programs does your department have with mental health organizations, and how does this collaboration inform the department's approach to crisis situations?

Citizens

1. How can you access information about the use of force policies and statistics of your local police department?
2. How transparent is your police department about instances of force, and are there public reports or databases available?
3. What training do officers in your community receive to handle high-pressure situations, particularly those involving mental health crises?
4. How are less-lethal options integrated into police use of force at your department, and under what circumstances are they used?
5. What percent of police officers in your local police department have completed Crisis Intervention Training?
6. What percent of police officers in your local police department have completed Mental Health First Aid training?

PRINCIPLE #7

*To maintain at all times a relationship with the public that gives reality to the historic tradition that the police are the **public** and that the public are the **police**, the police being only members of the public who are **paid** to give full time attention to duties which are incumbent on **every** citizen in the interests of community welfare and existence.*

The historical view of policing as a role centered around brute force and control starkly contrasts the evolved concept of community engagement and cooperative policing. Sir Robert Peel's vision in 1829 for a reciprocal relationship between the public and the police was groundbreaking, setting the stage for what has become a cornerstone of modern law enforcement.

Today, the relationship between the police and the community is a fundamental aspect of effective law enforcement. The necessity of this relationship goes beyond mere understanding; it is ingrained in the fabric of policing strategies. Officers who foster positive relationships within their communities often find greater success in maintaining peace and preventing crime. This community-oriented approach enhances the police's ability to solve problems collaboratively and increases the community's willingness to assist in policing efforts.

The statement *"the police are the public and the public are the police"* encapsulates the essence of this partnership. It suggests that police officers are not separate from their community but are integral members of it. This philosophy advocates for a partnership where the police and the public work together, leveraging diverse perspectives and resources for the greater good.

Modern policing strategies incorporate this principle by promoting transparency, accountability, and community involvement. Community policing, neighborhood watch, and police-youth initiatives are tangible expressions of this philosophy. Such programs build trust and empower community members to take an active role in their safety, creating a shared sense of responsibility.

The success of these collaborative efforts often hinges on the police force's ability to reflect the diversity of its community. Diversity within the police force enhances understanding and communication and fosters respect and mutual trust. This inclusivity is pivotal in addressing the unique challenges and needs of varied communities.

In the 21st century, integrating technology into policing—such as social media for communication, body-worn cameras for accountability, and data analysis for resource allocation—further supports this collaborative model. Technology can bridge gaps, provide insights, and create channels for dialogue and feedback that were not previously possible.

Peel's early recognition of the importance of public relations in policing was visionary. The evolution of this concept over the centuries has proven its value, recognizing the undeniable fact that law enforcement cannot operate in isolation from the community it serves. Modern law enforcement aims to maintain public safety through a partnership with the community, built on a solid foundation of trust, cooperation, and shared responsibility.

Building trust and mutual respect between the police and the community is an enduring principle that underpins the philosophy of modern policing. The essence of Sir Robert Peel's insight—that the police are an extension of the public and the public plays an integral role in law enforcement—is as relevant today as it was in the 19th century. This principle emphasizes the symbiotic relationship between law enforcement agencies and their communities.

Transparency and accountability are cornerstones of trust. Law enforcement agencies that commit to these values help to build confidence in their operations. The advent of body-worn cameras, open data initiatives, and civilian oversight are just a few examples of the efforts made to ensure police actions are visible and reviewable by the public.

The proactive engagement of communities in crime prevention and problem-solving reflects a shift from a reactive policing model to one that is preventive and collaborative. Police agencies are fostering this shift by creating forums for community dialogue, establishing joint problem-solving task forces, and encouraging community policing efforts.

The modern concept of policing also includes empowering the public. Citizens with the right tools and knowledge can become force multipliers in maintaining public safety. Law enforcement agencies actively promote citizen involvement through education programs, community workshops, and crime prevention campaigns.

Diversity within police forces is not just a matter of representation but a functional necessity for effective policing. Diverse law enforcement personnel bring many perspectives and experiences that enhance understanding and interactions within varied communities. This diversity strengthens community relations and helps provide more culturally responsive and sensitive services.

In line with Peel's principle, law enforcement today acknowledges that safety is a communal responsibility. The concept of the police are the public, and the public are the police reminds us that every citizen and officer has a role in crime prevention and community well-being. It's a call to unity, emphasizing that the foundation of a safe society is built on the collective efforts of all its members, with policing services acting as guardians of democratic values and human rights. This unity is achieved when police and the public work together in the spirit of trust, respect, and shared objectives.

This principle also reflects a fundamental truth in community policing: the police force is an integral part of the community it serves, and its effectiveness is deeply entwined with the community's participation and support. Sir Robert Peel's vision highlights the reciprocal nature of policing—a concept that modern law enforcement continues to embrace and promote.

Historically, the proximity of police officers to their communities was a given, with officers often living among the people they served. This closeness fostered a sense of camaraderie and mutual investment in the community's well-being. It allowed officers to know their neighborhoods intimately, understand the local dynamics and build relationships based on mutual trust and respect.

Over time, however, societal changes have influenced where police officers live and how they interact with their communities. The advent of modern transportation and the changing socioeconomic landscape have led to officers living farther from their beats. This shift, gradual at first, has had complex implications. Factors such as housing affordability, educational opportunities, personal safety concerns, and a desire for separation between work and personal life have all played a role in this evolution.

Despite these changes, the idea that officers should be closely connected to their communities has persisted. Residency requirements in the 1970s and '80s attempted to maintain this connection by legally mandating that police officers live in the cities where they worked. These requirements were seen as a way to ensure that officers had a vested interest in their communities, which could lead to more responsive and empathetic policing.[69]

Today, the debate over residency requirements continues, with some arguing that they help maintain community ties. In contrast, others believe they may be too restrictive and limit the pool of qualified applicants. Regardless of where officers reside, community engagement and partnership principles remain central to effective policing. The need for officers to build trust, understand community concerns, and work collaboratively with citizens is more important than ever.

Communities United Against Police Brutality, a Minneapolis-based organization, posits that their research has yet to find evidence to support the idea that residency requirements improve policing outcomes. *"Throughout our research, we have never encountered a shred of evidence that requiring or incentivizing police officers to live in the communities in which they work has any positive effect on the quality of policing."*[70]

[69] "Race and Police Brutality: Roots of an Urban Dilemma," Institute for Research on Poverty, University of Wisconsin-Madison, accessed June 3, 2023, https://www.irp. wisc.edu/publications/dps/pdfs/dp63680.pdf.

[70] "How police residency affects law enforcement and communities: The data," USA Today, accessed June 3, 2023, https://www.usatoday.com/story/news/nation/ 2020/06/13/police-residency-data/5327640002/.

According to a 2017 report, only eight percent of Minneapolis police officers lived within the city.[71] Similar rates are prevalent in other cities across the nation. About 15 percent of the Lansing Police Department officers live in the city, while the Ann Arbor Police Department has a residency rate of about 10 percent for police officers.[72]

Residency requirements for police officers continue to be a topic of debate, balancing community integration with recruitment challenges. Officers residing within their jurisdictions could improve community relations and increase investment in local issues. However, the viability of such requirements is complex.

Economic factors play a significant role in this complexity. High living costs can deter officers from residing within city limits in many urban areas. Housing prices, often inflated in metropolitan areas, can be prohibitive for officers whose salaries may not match the cost of living. This economic barrier poses a considerable challenge to enforcing residency requirements.

Additionally, concerns extend beyond finances. The social implications of being recognized while off duty can create discomfort for officers and their families. This visibility can lead to safety concerns and reluctance to engage in the community outside of professional responsibilities.

The implications for recruitment and retention are also substantial. As former Detriot Police Chief James Craig notes, residency requirements could narrow the field of potential recruits, limiting the diversity and skill set of the police force. This limitation could have far-reaching effects on departmental effectiveness and community relations.[73]

As law enforcement agencies grapple with these challenges, alternative strategies to residency requirements should be considered. These might include offering housing stipends, promoting community engagement

[71] "Few Minneapolis cops live inside city limits," Star Tribune, accessed June 3, 2023, https://www.startribune.com/few-minneapolis-cops-live-inside-city-limits/441581413/.

[72] "Reexamining Residency Rules for Detroit Police Officers," Crain's Detroit Business, accessed June 3, 2023, https://www.crainsdetroit.com/crains-forum/reexamining-residency-rules-detroit-police-officers.

[73] ibid

through other means, or developing programs encouraging officers to participate in community events, regardless of their residence.

Ultimately, the goal should be to find a balance that allows for meaningful community engagement without imposing undue hardships on officers or limiting the scope of potential recruits. By exploring creative solutions and maintaining a dialogue with community stakeholders, law enforcement agencies can work towards fostering positive relations between the police and the communities they serve, irrespective of where the officers call home.

In the City of Dunwoody, the innovative approach of offering a housing stipend to its police officers is a forward-thinking model to encourage residency within their jurisdiction. This initiative not only aids in recruitment by making the city a more financially viable option for officers, but it also fosters a sense of community engagement and availability in times of crisis.

In 2009, the Dunwoody Police Department began operations and offered a $300 housing stipend to help attract high-quality officers. Today, the housing stipend has risen to $800 a month.

The substantial increase in the housing stipend over nearly a decade and a half highlight the city's commitment to this strategy. The fact that 35 percent of the force resides within city limits is a testament to the program's success.

The policy of providing take-home vehicles adds another layer of community presence and rapid response capability. This not only ensures officers are seen as an integral part of the community but also contributes to a more visible police presence, which can deter crime. The financial savings from the housing stipend might also offset the costs associated with the take-home car program, indicating a thoughtful allocation of department resources.

Moreover, this approach can lead to stronger relationships between police officers and community members. When officers are seen as neighbors, not just enforcers, it can break down barriers and build trust. This trust is crucial for effective community policing, as residents may feel more comfortable reporting crime, sharing information, or working with the police on local initiatives.

Trust is the cornerstone of effective policing. When police officers live in the same neighborhoods as the residents they serve, it fosters a sense of camaraderie and mutual understanding. Officers become more attuned to the community's pulse, gaining firsthand insights into its dynamics, challenges, and aspirations. This proximity breaks down barriers and facilitates open communication channels, allowing residents to perceive law enforcement officers not merely as authority figures but as neighbors and allies committed to their well-being.

Living within the jurisdiction naturally translates into quicker response times during emergencies. When an officer resides nearby, they can swiftly address urgent situations, offering timely assistance and intervention. Moreover, community involvement means officers are more accessible to residents outside of crisis scenarios. They become familiar faces at local events, schools, and neighborhood gatherings, making it easier for citizens to approach them with concerns, inquiries, or even just for a friendly conversation.

Communities are diverse tapestries, each with a distinct culture, demographics, and socioeconomic landscape. Police officers who call these neighborhoods home gain invaluable insights into these nuances. They understand the streets' pulse, daily life rhythms, and the underlying issues affecting residents. This nuanced understanding empowers officers to tailor their policing strategies to suit the specific needs and sensitivities of the community, thereby fostering more effective crime prevention and resolution efforts.

Police officers serve as role models and pillars of authority within their communities. By residing locally, they embody a commitment to the neighborhoods they serve, setting a powerful example for residents, particularly impressionable youth.

When children see officers actively engaged in community affairs through volunteering, mentoring, or simply being present, it instills a sense of trust, respect, and aspiration. These interactions lay the groundwork for positive relationships between law enforcement and future generations, helping to shape a more harmonious and cohesive society.

For police officers, the job demands can be physically and emotionally taxing. Long commutes only exacerbate these challenges, eating into valuable time spent with family, pursuing personal interests, or engaging with the community.

By residing within the jurisdiction where they work, officers can enjoy a better work-life balance, reducing stress and fatigue associated with lengthy daily commutes. Additionally, it can lead to cost savings on transportation expenses, allowing officers to allocate resources toward other aspects of their lives.

The advantages of having police officers live in the communities they serve extend far beyond mere convenience. It is a strategic investment in building stronger, safer, and more cohesive neighborhoods. By bridging the gap between law enforcement and the community, fostering trust, enhancing responsiveness, and promoting positive role modeling, this approach lays the groundwork for more effective and equitable policing practices.

The Dunwoody model may inspire other departments grappling with the challenges of residency and community policing. As each city and department has unique needs and resources, tailored solutions like Dunwoody's housing stipend can offer a viable alternative to mandatory residency requirements. The success of such programs can lead to a more engaged, responsive, and community-oriented police force, which benefits both the officers and the citizens they serve.

As we navigate the complexities of modern society, the imperative to cultivate meaningful connections between police officers and the communities they serve remains as vital as ever. We can forge a future where safety, justice, and unity prevail through shared residency and collective engagement.

Having officers who live in the city where they serve and engage with their fellow citizens reflects the principle that Peel first penned in 1829: the police are the public.

The public are the police is the other half of the famous principle that the police are the public. Sir Robert Peel's assertion underlines that law enforcement is not an entity separate from the community but an integral part of it. Citizens share the responsibility for their community's welfare, safety, and security. Peel's vision emphasizes the collective role in maintaining order and preventing crime.

In today's context, this philosophy translates into various community engagement and partnership initiatives between the public and the police. Citizens are encouraged to participate in their safety by participating in community-based programs that align closely with law enforcement efforts.

The Neighborhood Watch program, initiated by the National Sheriff's Association in 1972 after a surge in crime during the 1960s, is one such program that exemplifies Peel's principle. It empowers residents to become extra eyes and ears for reporting suspicious activities, fostering a proactive approach to crime prevention. By working in tandem with local law enforcement, community members can contribute to deterring crime and increasing safety.[74]

Moving forward, the Neighborhood Watch program spread across the country. The Neighborhood Watch program is the largest and most successful citizen mobilization initiative ever introduced.

For example, the Dunwoody Police Department has 76 neighborhoods participating in their Neighborhood Watch program. Active members monitor their community and call 9-1-1 when they see something suspicious.

After all, the police can't be everywhere.

In one Dunwoody neighborhood, a male walking into the backyard of a home sparked a call to 9-1-1 from an active neighborhood watch participant. After a lengthy foot chase through the area, the suspect was arrested and charged with attempted burglary.

Undoubtedly, this arrest would not have happened without citizens' participation in their community's welfare, even though they aren't getting paid for their service.

What a great example of this principle at work!

Another critical community program is the Citizen Police Academy. It epitomizes the adage that the public are the police. Initially developed in the United Kingdom as a police night school, the program aimed to demystify police work and encourage community members to take a more active and informed role in public safety.[75]

In the United States and many other parts of the world, Citizen Police Academies have become a staple of community policing strategies.

[74] "What is Neighborhood Watch?" National Neighborhood Watch, accessed June 3, 2023, https://www.nnw.org/what-neighborhood-watch.

[75] "Citizen Police Academy," Town of Mount Pleasant Police Department, accessed June 3, 2023, https://www.tompsc.com/177/Citizen-Police-Academy#:~:text=History%20of%20the%20Citizen%20Police%20Academy&text=It%20began%20in%20the%20Devon,the%20City%20of%20Exeter%2C%20England.&text=In%201985%2C%20the%20Orlando%2C%20Florida,CPA)%20in%20the%20United%20States.

The Orlando Police Department was the first to bring this concept to the United States in 1985, hosting the first-ever Citizen Police Academy.[76]

These programs offer civilians a glimpse into the complexities of police work through a series of classes and interactive sessions. They cover various aspects of law enforcement, including criminal law, patrol procedures, investigations, community policing, and use of force policies. By providing this insight, citizens gain a deeper understanding of the daily decision-making processes and challenges that officers face.

Beyond education, Citizen Police Academies build stronger community relationships. They foster empathy and communication between police and residents, which can dispel misconceptions and build trust. Graduates of these academies often become ambassadors for the police within their communities, sharing their knowledge and experiences with neighbors, friends, and family.

Citizen Police Academies also serve as a feedback mechanism for law enforcement agencies. Through open dialogue, police can hear directly from citizens about their concerns, ideas, and perceptions. This feedback can be invaluable in shaping policies, training, and strategies that are more responsive to the community's needs.

The academies typically culminate in a graduation ceremony, marking the participants' program completion and often leading to the formation of alumni groups. These groups may continue to engage with the police department in various capacities, such as volunteering, organizing community events, or participating in advisory committees.

The Citizen Police Academy reflects a commitment to community-oriented policing and public partnership. It's an educational tool that empowers citizens to become more proactive in their safety and enhances the overall effectiveness of policing through community collaboration.

This proactive, educational approach to policing embodies Peel's principles. It acknowledges that an informed and engaged citizenry is crucial to maintaining public peace and the effectiveness of the police. As communities evolve and new challenges emerge, programs like the Citizen

---

76 Office of Justice Programs (OJP), "Community Citizen Police Academies," accessed May 31, 2023, https://www.ojp.gov/ncjrs/virtual-library/abstracts/community-citizen-police-academies.

Police Academy will remain vital in cultivating informed, cooperative, and safety-conscious communities.

Most police departments are understaffed and certainly can't be everywhere all the time. Therefore, citizens need to call 9-1-1 when they see something suspicious or out of the ordinary.

The phrase "*If you see something, say something*" encapsulates a fundamental shift in public safety messaging that emphasizes the critical role of the community in security efforts. Conceived by Allen Kay in the wake of the September 11, 2001, attacks on a note card, this slogan became more than just a catchphrase; it represented a call to action for every citizen to become an active participant in the collective security of their community.[77]

The New York Metropolitan Transportation Authority (MTA) adoption of this phrase in 2002 marked the beginning of a nationwide campaign that would eventually be embraced by numerous agencies, including the Department of Homeland Security, who adopted the phrase to fight terrorism.[78] It encouraged citizens to report suspicious behavior or items vulnerable to potential threats, particularly in public spaces and transit systems.

This public safety initiative rests on the premise that law enforcement officers cannot be everywhere at once. Therefore, community vigilance can play a crucial role in preventing crime and terrorism. It is an appeal to the shared responsibility of citizens to look out for one another and to act as the eyes and ears of law enforcement.

The effectiveness of this slogan lies in its simplicity and the empowerment it offers to the average person. Providing a clear and straightforward directive removes ambiguity about what to do when confronted with a potential threat. It also fosters a sense of agency among community members, reminding them that their actions can significantly impact public safety.

---

[77] "How 'If you see something, say something' became our national motto," The Washington Post, accessed June 3, 2023, https://www.washingtonpost.com/posteverything/wp/2016/09/23/how-if-you-see-something-say-something-became-our-national-motto/.

[78] "If You See Something, Say Something™ Campaign Overview," Department of Homeland Security, accessed June 3, 2023, https://www.dhs.gov/publication/if-you-see-something-say-something™-campaign-overview.

Moreover, if you see something, say something is a saying that aligns seamlessly with community policing models. It encourages open communication between the public and law enforcement, leading to quicker responses to suspicious activities and preventing incidents before they occur. This partnership helps build trust and reinforces the concept that safety is a shared concern, requiring everyone's participation.

In the years following its introduction, the phrase has been adopted in various forms across different sectors, from airports to schools. It has been integrated into public awareness campaigns, safety drills, and educational programs. Its resonance with the public demonstrates the power of community involvement and the importance of collective vigilance in maintaining a safe society.

The enduring legacy of this simple yet profound phrase is a testament to the importance of community engagement in policing. It underscores the notion that while law enforcement is a dedicated guardian of public safety, every citizen plays a vital role in creating a secure environment. As communities continue to navigate the complexities of modern threats, the spirit of this message remains a guiding force in fostering collaborative efforts to protect our shared spaces.

In a world often divided by tensions between law enforcement and communities, Reverend Markel Hutchins, who was mentioned previously, emerged as a beacon of hope, dedicating his efforts to bridging the gap and fostering unity. His visionary leadership led to the creation of the Faith and Blue Weekend, a transformative event that aims to bring police officers and communities together.[79]

Reverend Markel Hutchins, an influential figure in his Atlanta community, recognized the urgent need to address the strained relationship between law enforcement and marginalized communities. Witnessing the erosion of trust and the widening divide, he sought to bridge this gap and restore harmony through the power of faith. Hutchins understood that faith-based initiatives could play a pivotal role in fostering understanding, empathy, and reconciliation.

---

[79] Community Oriented Policing Services (COPS) Office, "National Faith and Blue Weekend," accessed May 31, 2023, https://cops.usdoj.gov/html/dispatch/11-2020/national_faith_and_blue_weekend.html.

Motivated by the belief that true transformation can only occur through open and honest conversations, Hutchins collaborated with local law enforcement agencies and faith-based organizations to develop a weekend of activities promoting positive interactions and deeper connections. Participants engage in meaningful exchanges through sports, community service projects, workshops, and shared meals, dispelling misconceptions and fostering empathy.

The impact of Reverend Hutchins' Faith and Blue Weekend extends far beyond the event itself. The initiative serves as a catalyst for ongoing community engagement and dialogue throughout the year. It inspires local leaders, faith-based organizations, and community members to work collaboratively to address systemic issues, build bridges, and promote social justice.

Moreover, Faith and Blue Weekend's success has garnered national attention. By sharing their experiences and best practices, communities nationwide are leveraging Reverend Hutchins' vision to break down barriers and heal the divisions plaguing society.

Although the previously discussed programs and various others have made it easy for citizens to be involved in their community and with their police department, there is still a disconnect in some communities.

As previously discussed, the tragic death of George Floyd ignited a national reckoning, highlighting the deep-seated mistrust between law enforcement and particularly communities of color.

This event, and others like it, are stark reminders of the long shadow cast by historical injustices, such as the slave patrols that once enforced brutal laws against African Americans. These patrols are a memorable part of the history that informs today's complex relationship between the police and the communities they serve.[80]

Many people are willing to believe the worst about the police.

The shift towards stark professionalism within law enforcement in the 1950s, exemplified by the iconic phrase from Dragnet, *"Just the facts, ma'am,"* marked a significant change in policing philosophy. This

---

80   "Law Enforcement Must Regain the Public's Trust," Police Foundation, accessed June 3, 2023, https://www.policefoundation.org/law-enforcement-must-regain-the-publics-trust/?gclid=Cj0KCQiAyJOBBhDCARIsAJG2h5erW1gLLpum_ovQZ6FdY9JrUKCShZ42zwumxPajssk75UdVYhZYNgcaAjEkEALw_wcB.

era focused on factual evidence and a systematic approach to law enforcement, sidelining the importance of relationships and community connections in policing.

However, the subsequent decade revealed the limitations of this approach. The civil rights movement of the 1960s exposed deep fractures between law enforcement and communities of color. Images of police dogs, water hoses, and batons used against peaceful protesters demanding equal rights remain a dark testament to this period.[81]

These acts did not just enforce segregation laws; they etched a legacy of fear and mistrust that has persisted over generations. The overemphasis on *"professionalism"* and *"facts"* failed to account for the need for justice, empathy, and community collaboration.

This treatment of African Americans and the subsequent distancing of the police from people of color underscored a critical flaw in law enforcement: the lack of understanding and respect for the communities they were meant to protect and serve. The *"us versus them"* mentality that became prevalent during this time did more than just alienate; it sowed seeds of discord that have grown into systemic challenges faced by modern policing.

Then, in 1991, the Rodney King beating at the hands of Los Angeles police officers, captured on video, was not just a moment of grievous police misconduct but a profound symbol of systemic issues within law enforcement. The video footage made public the kind of brutality that many African Americans had long reported but which had often been dismissed or ignored by the broader society.[82]

This incident did not stand alone; it became a powerful validation of the lived experiences of minorities with law enforcement and was seared into the national consciousness as emblematic of a much larger problem.

The reaction to the Rodney King video was not just about the beating itself; it was a response to the historical accumulation of similar, unacknowledged incidents. It brought to the forefront the urgent need for police reform and establishing accountability measures. The ensuing public outcry and civil unrest in Los Angeles laid bare the deep chasm of distrust between law enforcement and minority communities.

---

[81]   ibid

[82]   ibid

The King incident acted as a catalyst for change, driving the advancement of community policing models to rebuild trust and foster collaboration between the police and the communities they serve. It emphasized the importance of cultural competence training, de-escalation tactics, and reevaluating use-of-force policies.

Even now, decades later, the legacy of the Rodney King beating informs discussions about police practices and the movement for social justice. It reminds us that the road to reform is ongoing and that creating a just and fair policing system requires constant vigilance, community engagement, and an unwavering commitment to upholding the rights and dignity of all individuals.

Reforming policing practices to restore trust must acknowledge this history and its continuing impact. Law enforcement agencies need to move beyond just facts and procedures to a more holistic approach that values relationships, understands cultural nuances, and respects the dignity of every individual, irrespective of their race or background.

Community-oriented policing, which encourages positive interactions between officers and the communities they serve, and sensitivity training that includes the historical context of policing can help mend these fractures. By integrating the lessons of the past into contemporary policing strategies, law enforcement can work towards a future where public safety is a collaborative effort and justice is served with compassion and respect for all citizens.

The painful lessons of the past must inform future policies, ensuring that no community feels targeted or alienated by those sworn to protect them. Only by embracing a philosophy that values facts and relationships can law enforcement hope to rebuild the trust essential for a safe and equitable society.

Of course, trust is the lifeblood of community policing, serving as the fundamental basis upon which effective law enforcement and community partnerships are built. Without trust, the delicate fabric of community cooperation unravels, leaving law enforcement agencies unable to serve and protect effectively. Various studies have consistently shown that when trust in the police increases, so does the community's willingness to cooperate, leading to a symbiotic relationship that enhances the safety and well-being of all.

The research underscores the correlation between trust and cooperation. Communities with high trust in their police force are more likely to report crimes, offer vital information, and work collaboratively with officers to address local issues.[83] This cooperation is crucial for crime prevention and solving, creating a proactive environment where the police and the community are actively engaged in safeguarding their neighborhoods.

Conversely, the absence of trust creates a barrier to effective law enforcement. When communities harbor suspicion or fear towards the police, they become less inclined to engage with officers, report crimes, or contribute to law enforcement efforts. This lack of cooperation can damage policing initiatives, allowing criminal activities to go unchecked and undermining the safety of the community.

Building and maintaining trust is multifaceted, requiring consistent effort, open communication, and mutual respect. It involves law enforcement agencies being transparent in their operations, accountable for their actions, and responsive to the community's concerns. It also entails the community being receptive, supportive, and active participants in public safety initiatives.

Building trust is an ongoing process that must be nurtured continuously through dialogue, collaboration, and shared goals. The benefits of this trust are immeasurable, leading to safer communities, more effective policing, and a strengthened social fabric that can withstand the challenges of a dynamic society. For community policing to reach its full potential, trust must be prioritized, cultivated, and preserved as an essential element of the partnership between the police and the public they serve.

In 2015, the Police Executive Research Forum (PERF) hosted one of its national meetings to bring together police leaders and community leaders to discuss building trust between the police and the community.[84]

---

[83]   "What Happens When We Don't Trust Law Enforcement?" Psychology Today, accessed June 3, 2023, https://www.psychologytoday.com/us/blog/brick-brick/201409/what-happens-when-we-dont-trust-law-enforcement-0.

[84]   "Improving Police-Community Relations: A Report from the Department of Justice's Community Relations Service," Department of Justice, accessed June 3, 2023, https://www.justice.gov/crs/file/836486/download.

The results of the meeting provide a modern-day roadmap for the police to be the public and the public to be the police, working together in a high-trust environment.

PERF identified five recommendations.

1. Acknowledge and discuss the challenges you are facing with your community.

Having a dialogue to talk about important issues is critical. There is a reason this recommendation is first.

Excessive use of force by a police officer in another agency far away can have repercussions locally, even though the local agency was not involved. These failures by law enforcement in one jurisdiction serve as a reminder of the past mistreatment of citizens.

Law enforcement leaders have taken significant steps in recent years to acknowledge people of color's historical mistreatment.

As mentioned, the International Association of Chiefs of Police (IACP) President Terry Cunningham delivered a powerful speech in 2016. He publicly recognized the documented unfair treatment of communities of color by law enforcement in the past.[85] President Cunningham apologized for this past treatment.

Similarly, Chief Robert Murphy of the Montgomery Police Department apologized in 2013 to Congressman John Lewis for an attack on the Freedom Riders and John Lewis in 1961. Chief Murphy even presented his badge to Congressman Lewis.[86]

Chief Murphy's public apology to Congressman Lewis came decades after the Freedom Rides, a series of nonviolent protests that aimed to challenge racial segregation in interstate transportation during the early 1960s.

---

[85] "Head of Police Chiefs Group Apologizes for 'Historical Mistreatment' of Minorities," NPR, accessed June 3, 2023, https://www.npr.org/sections/thetwo-way/2016/10/18/498380373/head-of-police-chiefs-group-apologizes-for-historical-mistreatment-of-minorities.

[86] "Montgomery (Alabama) Police Chief Lauded for Apology, Giving Badge," Officer.com, accessed June 3, 2023, https://www.officer.com/home/news/10891220/montgomery-alabama-police-chief-lauded-for-apology-giving-badge.

The Freedom Riders, comprising both black and white activists, faced brutal violence and unjust treatment as they journeyed through the South.

Chief Murphy's apology carries immense symbolism and signifies the evolution of societal attitudes. By acknowledging the wrongdoing of the past, Chief Murphy demonstrates a willingness to confront the dark chapters of history and move towards a more inclusive and compassionate future.

Chief Murphy's heartfelt apology to Congressman John Lewis for the mistreatment of the Freedom Riders is a powerful and necessary step toward reconciliation and healing. It acknowledges the suffering endured by those who fought for civil rights and honors their indomitable spirit in the face of adversity.

His apology paves the way for dialogue, understanding, and progress as society strives toward a more inclusive and just future. As we reflect upon this apology, we are reminded of the importance of acknowledging past wrongs, rectifying them, and building bridges to create a more compassionate society.

In 2017, Chief Lou Dekmar of the LaGrange Police Department delivered inspiring remarks at a Warren Temple United Methodist Church gathering. Chief Dekmar said, *"As LaGrange police chief, I sincerely regret and denounce the role our police department played in Austin's lynching, both through our action and inaction. For that, I'm profoundly sorry. It should never have happened."*[87]

Chief Dekmar's remarks related to the arrest of a 16-year-old African American teenager in 1940. A local lynch mob took Austin from the jail, and his body was found soon after, riddled with bullets. LaGrange police officers did not stop the crowd, nor did they investigate Austin's death.

Chief Dekmar's apology for the death of Austin Calloway should not be seen as the endpoint but rather as the beginning of a transformative process. It is a call to action for police departments across the nation to reassess their practices, policies, and approaches to policing communities of color.

Law enforcement agencies can work towards eliminating systemic biases and building stronger relationships with their communities by

---

[87] "In Apology For Decades-Old Lynching, Police Chief Aims To 'Interrupt The Past'," NPR, accessed June 3, 2023, https://www.npr.org/sections/thetwo-way/2017/01/27/512036362/in-apology-for-decades-old-lynching-police-chief-aims-to-interrupt-the-past.

prioritizing community engagement, cultural sensitivity, and de-escalation training. Furthermore, it is imperative to establish robust mechanisms for accountability and oversight to ensure that incidents like the death of Austin Calloway never happen again.

2. Be transparent and accountable.

In the ever-evolving landscape of law enforcement, transparency is no longer optional; it is essential for fostering trust and legitimacy within the community. While certain operations and investigations require confidentiality to ensure effectiveness and officer safety, the overarching activities of the police should be visible and understandable to the public they serve.

A practical transparency model involves timely information dissemination, particularly after critical incidents. This openness reassures the public that the department is acting with integrity and is willing to be held accountable. In the digital age, having department policies and procedures readily accessible online allows for public awareness and understanding of law enforcement protocols.

The commitment to transparency extends beyond reactive measures; it includes proactive data sharing. Many modern police departments now utilize online platforms to publish crime statistics, maps, and annual reports. These tools inform the public and invite community input, creating a feedback loop that can drive policy and operational changes.

Moreover, transparency is a catalyst for building trust. It dismantles the barriers of suspicion and fosters a collaborative spirit between the police and the community. Trust is further solidified when the public sees that their law enforcement agencies are open to scrutiny and responsive to community concerns.

Embracing transparency also means embracing technology. Digital platforms can serve as conduits for information sharing, where the public can track crime trends, understand resource deployment, and monitor the outcomes of community policing initiatives. These platforms can also facilitate dialogue, where questions can be asked and answered in public forums, promoting a culture of openness and inclusivity.

Incorporating transparency into daily operations requires a cultural shift within police departments. It necessitates training officers to understand the importance of open communication and equipping them with the skills to engage with the public effectively.

Transparency is about building a relationship based on trust, respect, and mutual understanding. It is about creating a community where everyone feels safe, heard, and valued. By adopting a transparent approach, police departments affirm their dedication to serving the public interest and upholding democratic values.

The journey towards transparency and accountability is ongoing. It is a commitment to continuous improvement, listening and responding to community needs, and operating in a manner that reflects the values of the society they protect. As police departments embrace this journey, they enhance their credibility and contribute to the greater social good, reinforcing the fundamental principle that the police are the public and the public are the police.

Recently, the Dunwoody Police Department created a Transparency & Data Sharing Initiative page on their website. Citizens have access to the department's policies, crime data, use of force data, complaints, demographics, turnover rate, and other vital data.[88]

The Dunwoody Police Department's Transparency & Data Sharing Initiative is an exemplary proactive communication and community relations model. It reflects an understanding that effective policing is not done to a community but with a community. By fostering a climate of openness, the initiative aligns with the foundational principles of democratic policing, paving the way for stronger community-police relations and enhanced public safety.

In a world increasingly laser-focused on law enforcement's conduct, the onus on police leaders to uphold stringent accountability standards is profound. A police department's integrity and the public's perception of its credibility hinge on the consistent application of transparent disciplinary processes that match community expectations and resonate with the department's internal policies.

---

[88] "Dunwoody Police Department Launches Transparency Portal," Appen Media Group, accessed June 3, 2023, https://www.appenmedia.com/dunwoody/dunwoody-police-department-launches-transparency-portal/article_0f48320e-0555-11ee-950c-5fe761a0b504.html.

When police leaders ensure accountability within their ranks, they maintain and often enhance the community's trust. This trust is the bedrock of effective policing, fostering cooperation and open communication between officers and the citizens they serve. By holding officers accountable, police departments clearly communicate that they operate in the public's best interest.

Accreditation and state certification, such as those granted by organizations like CALEA, are not mere accolades. They represent a commitment to professionalism and are a testament to a department's adherence to the best practices in law enforcement. Pursuing such recognition is a proactive declaration of a department's dedication to excellence and openness to scrutiny and improvement.

Ethical conduct within the police force is not optional; it's a mandate. Complaints against officers must be investigated rigorously, and subsequent disciplinary actions, if necessary, must be transparent. This ensures that officers remain within the ethical boundaries set forth by the profession, reinforcing a culture of integrity.

A police department facilitating an open and responsive complaint process invites its community to engage constructively. Citizens who believe their grievances will be fairly addressed are more likely to bring forward their concerns. This openness promotes a culture of accountability and ensures that police officers are protected from unwarranted accusations, maintaining a just balance within the department.

When applied, disciplinary measures must be consistent and proportionate to the actions being disciplined. This consistency fortifies the department's resolve to uphold high standards and deters other officers who might otherwise consider stepping out of line.

Addressing individual misconduct cases is the visible aspect of accountability, but on a deeper level, it allows police leaders to identify and rectify broader systemic issues within their departments. Such introspection and correction can lead to overall improvements in policing practices.

Moreover, an environment that encourages self-regulation is cultivated. Officers who are aware of the scrutiny their actions will undergo may become more reflective and prudent in their conduct and decision-making.

The reputation of a police department is crucial. One known for its rigorous accountability measures is viewed favorably by the community it serves and is seen as an attractive workplace for recruits serious about ethical policing.

The push for accountability transcends the act of discipline. It embodies a commitment to a fair, just, and community-centric approach to law enforcement. When departments engage in accreditation, transparent investigations, and fair disciplinary practices, they do more than serve the public. They honor the professional commitments of their officers and build a culture of mutual trust, respect, and partnership. This is the essence of democratic policing, a beacon that guides departments toward a future where community safety and harmony are paramount.

Unfortunately, the anti-police rhetoric of late has increased unsubstantiated complaints against police officers that must be sifted through.

3. Take steps to reduce bias and improve cultural competency.

In the quest for justice, law enforcement leaders are responsible for cultivating an environment where impartiality is the norm and bias is prohibited. While it is a commendable starting point to establish policies that prohibit discrimination, the true measure of commitment to these principles is found in the daily actions and decisions of those in supervisory roles. Enforcing these policies through decisive action when violations occur sends an unmistakable message throughout the ranks: bias, whether overt or subtle, will not be tolerated.

The crux of effective law enforcement hinges on the trust and cooperation of the community it serves. This trust is significantly bolstered when officers are trained to recognize and mitigate the influence of implicit biases. Such biases, woven into the fabric of human psychology, can unwittingly skew judgment and tarnish the fairness of policing if left unchecked.

Training programs like Fair and Impartial Policing are vital tools in the law enforcement arsenal, helping officers understand and navigate the undercurrents of implicit bias.[89] This training illuminates the subconscious prejudices that can seep into decision-making, providing strategies to ensure that these biases do not compromise the integrity of law enforcement actions.

---

[89] "FIPolicing," accessed June 3, 2023, https://fipolicing.com/.

The benefits of this training extend beyond the individual officer; they permeate the entire department, fostering a culture of integrity and fairness. Moreover, they resonate within the community, demonstrating a commitment to just and equitable policing. As officers learn to prevent biases from influencing their work, they enhance their professionalism and build stronger, more trusting, and cooperative relationships with the communities they are sworn to protect.

Law enforcement agencies that prioritize bias awareness and actively engage in such training are poised to set new benchmarks for fairness in policing. They position themselves at the forefront of progressive law enforcement, leading by example and setting a standard for others.

The journey toward fair and impartial policing is ongoing and multifaceted. It requires the steadfast dedication of police leaders to enforce non-discriminatory policies and the willingness of officers to engage in continuous learning and self-reflection. By embracing these challenges, law enforcement can forge a path of respect, trust, and mutual understanding that upholds the fundamental tenets of justice and equality.

4. Maintain focus on the importance of collaboration and be visible in the community.

The tapestry of community safety is woven from the threads of law enforcement's responses to calls for service or enforcement actions and the rich hues of relationships between the police and the community they serve. These relationships are the bedrock upon which trust is built, understanding is fostered, and sustainable community well-being is developed.

The essence of relationship building within community policing lies in the everyday, seemingly small interactions between a police officer and a community member. It is in the friendly exchange between an officer and a local shopkeeper, the conversation with a worried parent, or the reassuring presence at a community event. These micro-level interactions, though fleeting, accumulate to form the foundation of trust and cooperation necessary for effective policing.

Organized initiatives like neighborhood watch programs, citizen police academies, police athletic leagues, and citizen ride-a-longs serve as structured avenues for these exchanges. They offer a platform for police officers to step outside their traditional roles and engage with citizens in settings that promote mutual understanding.

Town hall meetings and community forums further expand this dialogue, providing a stage for open communication where concerns can be voiced, policies can be discussed, and collective goals can be set. Such forums allow the police to explain their strategies and actions, thus demystifying law enforcement processes and garnering community support.

These initiatives offer more than a glimpse into the lives and work of the police—they invite the community to participate actively in the safety and security of their neighborhoods. Through such partnerships, policing becomes a service provided to the community and a joint venture where every citizen and officer plays an integral role.

In this ever-evolving landscape of community relations, it is clear that the future of effective law enforcement is deeply intertwined with its ability to build and maintain positive, proactive relationships with the community. Through these collaborative efforts, policing transcends its traditional bounds and becomes a shared responsibility, a collective endeavor towards a safer, more harmonious society.

5. Promote internal diversity and ensure professional growth opportunities.

In the intricate weave of community fabric, diversity is not merely a thread but a vibrant pattern that enriches and strengthens the whole. The principle that the police are the public, and the public are the police illuminates the significance of this diversity within law enforcement agencies. Such agencies must reflect the kaleidoscopic nature of the communities they protect and serve. While a diverse workforce is not a panacea for all issues, it is a critical step toward cultivating improved relations between the police and the community.

Police departments that mirror the diversity of their communities foster an environment of inclusiveness and respect. It promotes understanding different cultures, languages, and perspectives, which is paramount in today's multifaceted societies. By recognizing the value of diversity, law enforcement agencies gain the community's trust and legitimacy and enhance their communication and effectiveness in policing.

Investing in a police force's professional growth is also a testament to the value placed on each staff member. Chief Bobby Moody's philosophy at the Marietta Police Department reflects this principle. As officers climb the ranks, the focus progressively shifts from personal development to fostering the growth of others. By the time an officer reaches the pinnacle of leadership, their role evolves into one dedicated to nurturing the department's collective expertise and potential.

This philosophy of nurturing growth cultivates a culture where officers feel appreciated and supported, influencing how they interact with the community. When officers are treated fairly and respectfully within their departments, it naturally extends outward in their dealings with citizens. Officers who perceive their work environment as just and equitable are more inclined to carry those principles into every community interaction, embodying the fairness they experience.

Thus, fostering diversity within the ranks and the commitment to professional development are not just strategies but foundational to the ethos of modern policing. They are integral to actualizing the vision that Sir Robert Peel articulated, ensuring that the police and public are not just allies in maintaining order but partners in achieving a shared vision of community wellbeing.

As departments navigate the complexities of law enforcement in the modern age, these principles serve as guiding stars. They ensure that the police force is not only a reflection of the community's diversity but also a proponent of its members' growth and development. In doing so, they uphold the promise that the police are indeed the public, and the public are the police—a covenant as enduring as the principle itself.

Following these five PERF suggestions is undoubtedly an excellent place to start restoring trust between the police and the local community.

Several years ago, the IACP kicked off its Trust Building Campaign, which sought to enhance trust between police agencies and the communities they serve.[90]

The Trust Building Campaign emerges as a vital endeavor. This initiative calls upon police agencies to commit to substantive changes across

---

[90]　International Association of Chiefs of Police (IACP), "IACP Trust Building Campaign," accessed May 31, 2023, https://www.theiacp.org/iacp-trust-building-campaign.

critical facets of policing. By pledging to adopt unbiased practices, refine use-of-force policies, cultivate leadership that underscores the value of community trust, and foster a culture that prizes diversity in recruitment, law enforcement can make significant strides toward mending and strengthening the ties with the public.[91]

The pressing need for trust between police and community is acknowledged universally across major law enforcement organizations. In today's climate, where skepticism and scrutiny of police are at an all-time high, establishing trust is more than a goal—it is required. The dwindling numbers of those drawn to the policing profession, alongside the departure of current officers, reflect a crisis not just in recruitment but in public perception.

The images and narratives that have flooded media outlets in recent years have left an indelible mark on the collective consciousness, painting a picture of a profession in turmoil. These narratives, often centered around high-profile incidents of police misconduct, have sown doubt and dissent, prompting many within the ranks to reconsider their call to duty.

Yet, despite these tribulations, the path to reconciliation and unity is illuminated by hope. For the chasm between police officers and the communities they serve to close a concerted, mutual effort is required—a commitment to dialog and understanding, to listening and empathy, transparency and action.

Building trust is not an overnight endeavor. It requires ongoing effort, a commitment to open communication, and a willingness to listen and learn from one another. It's about creating a culture where the police are the public, and the public are the police is not just a slogan but a lived reality. It is about fostering a community where officers are seen not just as enforcers of the law but as integral, trusted members of the very fabric they vow to protect.

The future of effective law enforcement hinges on the ability to cultivate these relationships. It calls for stepping beyond the traditional bounds of policing and into community partnership. When law enforcement agencies and the public join forces, driven by a shared vision of safety and respect, the principle Sir Robert Peel set forth over a century ago becomes tangible.

---

[91]   ibid

Peel's Principles in Practice: Questions for Today's Challenges and Opportunities

Police Officers

1. In what ways is your department ensuring that it reflects the diversity of the community you serve?
2. How does your department foster the concept that "the police are the public and the public are the police" in its day-to-day interactions?
3. In what ways does your department support officers living in or close to the community they serve?
4. Does your police department provide a housing stipend or other benefit for officers who live in its jurisdiction?
5. Does your police department participate in the Faith and Blue Weekend events? How about you?
6. How is your department promoting internal diversity and ensuring professional growth opportunities for all officers?
7. Does your police department hold a Citizen Police Academy?
8. Has your police department committed a historical wrong that has damaged the department's relationship with the community that might be repaired with a public apology?

Citizens

1. What measures are in place to ensure your police force is diverse and representative of your community's demographics?
2. How can you, as a citizen, contribute to and participate in policing efforts, such as neighborhood watch or police-youth initiatives?
3. Does your police department offer any incentives, such as housing stipends, to encourage officers to live within the community?
4. What percent of police officers in your local police department live in its jurisdiction?
5. What educational programs like Citizen Police Academies are available for citizens to learn more about policing?
6. How can you get involved in dialogues or forums with your police department to discuss community concerns and solutions?

PRINCIPLE #8

*To recognise always the need for **strict** adherence to police-executive functions, and to **refrain** from even seeming to **usurp** the powers of the judiciary of avenging individuals or the State, and of authoritatively **judging** guilt and **punishing** the guilty.*

Navigating the delicate balance of power within the criminal justice system requires a steadfast adherence to foundational principles. The tripartite structure, with the legislative, judiciary, and executive branches, embodies a framework designed to maintain equilibrium and fairness. This system ensures that no single branch wields undue influence throughout justice, safeguarding individual rights at every juncture.

Sir Robert Peel's eighth principle highlights the imperative for law enforcement to operate within the bounds of their designated role. In contemporary policing, this principle takes on added significance. It serves as a fortification against the misuse of power, reinforcing the notion that police officers are guardians of peace, tasked with preserving order and safeguarding the community's welfare.

In their role, police officers are vested with profound responsibilities: they enforce laws, they possess the authority to deprive individuals of their liberty through arrest, and under extenuating circumstances, they may be required to make life-and-death decisions. Such powers, while necessary, must be exercised with the utmost discretion and a profound sense of duty.

Adherence to Peel's tenet is about refraining from overstepping authority and nurturing public trust by embodying the virtues of justice and impartiality. Officers are urged to avoid any semblance of vigilantism to avoid assuming the roles of judge, jury, and executioner. In an age where narratives can be swiftly shaped by public opinion and media portrayal, law enforcement's actions must remain grounded in legality and ethical conduct, avoiding the pitfalls of personal retribution or extrajudicial penalties.

How can police agencies ensure they are operating professionally and following best practices?

In pursuing excellence and integrity within law enforcement, international accreditation and state certification emerge as powerful tools, symbolic of an agency's commitment to professional standards. Establishing the Commission on Accreditation for Law Enforcement Agencies (CALEA) in 1979 marked a significant stride towards this goal. Conceived with the collective insight and backing of the International Association of Chiefs of Police (IACP), the National Sheriffs Association (NSA), the National Organization of Black Law Enforcement Executives (NOBLE), and the Police Executive Research Forum (PERF), CALEA stands as a testament to the law enforcement community's aspiration for advancement and accountability.[92]

The essence of CALEA lies in its comprehensive set of standards designed to enhance law enforcement service delivery. These standards cover many operational and administrative aspects, including but not limited to the use of force, protection of citizen rights, vehicle pursuits, property and evidence handling, and recruitment processes. By subscribing to these benchmarks, police departments vow to uphold the law and elevate their service to the highest echelons of professionalism and responsiveness.[93]

---

[92]   "Commission on Accreditation for Law Enforcement Agencies (CALEA)," accessed June 3, 2023, https://www.calea.org/.

[93]   "CALEA Accreditation: A Platform for Excellence and Reform," Police Foundation, accessed June 3, 2023, https://www.policefoundation.org/calea-accreditation-a-platform-for-excellence-and-reform/?gclid=CjwKCAiAhbeCBhB-cEiwAkv2cYymtkJNIOZcupAah9FoMExns7EWppa_8okrVkso7d5HnMyX-jyRkVHRoCGIcQAvD_BwE.

CALEA's accreditation process is meticulous and multifaceted, involving self-assessments, on-site evaluations, community feedback, and commission reviews. This rigorous examination ensures that an agency's practices and policies align with legal requirements and modern policing principles that prioritize human dignity and community trust.

The benefits of accreditation include improving the relationship between the department and the community, greater accountability from supervisors, control of liability insurance costs, administrative improvements, increased governmental and community support, and the facilitation of the department's pursuit of excellence.[94]

In addition to CALEA, state certification programs offer another layer of validation, often tailored to address specific regional concerns and legal frameworks at a lower cost. These certifications mirror the rigorous standards of CALEA while also incorporating local statutes and community values, thus ensuring that law enforcement agencies operate under the best practices recognized by their states.

CALEA accreditation and state certification are cornerstones for building transparent, efficient, and community-focused law enforcement agencies. These programs symbolize a department's unwavering dedication to continuous improvement and public service. As the guardians of public safety, law enforcement agencies that engage in these processes fulfill their mandate and forge a path of trust and partnership with the communities they have sworn to protect and serve.

By engaging in these voluntary processes, law enforcement agencies demonstrate their resolve to exceed the baseline of satisfactory policing, opting instead to reach for the pinnacle of law enforcement excellence. The rigorous standards and expectations these accreditation and certification bodies set ensure that every aspect of policing is scrutinized and aligned with the principles of justice, transparency, and community service.

In an era where public scrutiny of police actions is at an all-time high, CALEA accreditation and state certification are more than just badges of

---

[94] "Accreditation 101: The Benefits of State and National Police Accreditation," Benchmark Analytics, accessed June 3, 2023, https://www.benchmarkanalytics.com/blog/accreditation-101-the-benefits-of-state-and-national-police-accreditation/#:~:text=The%20primary%20benefits%20of%20CALEA,and%20facilitation%20of%20an%20agency's.

honor; they are beacons of a department's resolve to foster trust, embrace accountability, and commit to continual improvement. As such, these processes are integral to the evolution of law enforcement, ensuring that the shield officers carry is not only a symbol of authority but also a covenant of public service and ethical responsibility.

While state certification and national accreditation ensure that police departments adhere to rigorous standards, fostering professionalism, accountability, and community trust, it is crucial to recognize the human side of policing.

Certification and accreditation cannot transform officers into infallible beings or avenging heroes. Rather, police officers are everyday individuals tasked with upholding the law under challenging and often dangerous circumstances. This reality highlights the importance of understanding their role within the boundaries of law and ethics, dispelling any misconceptions of them as vigilante figures, and instead appreciating their commitment to justice and community service.

In the rich history of modern cinema, the allure of the vigilante hero resonates deeply within popular culture. The cinematic universe has been graced by figures like the Avengers, superheroes who stand against evil, often bending the rules to dispense justice. This narrative thread weaves through the fabric of many stories, including the visceral tale of retribution in Death Wish, where Charles Bronson's character pursues the violent men who destroyed his family.

As these narratives unfold, they touch upon a raw nerve, the primal yearning for justice and the cathartic release of vengeance. Yet, these are stories of fiction, diverging from the tenets that govern our real world, particularly law enforcement and justice. In our society, vigilantism finds no refuge; the path of vengeance is not ours to walk. The principles that guide the police force are antithetical to the notion of taking justice into one's hands. Police officers are not Avengers. They are guardians bound by duty, law, and a profound respect for the rights enshrined in the Constitution.

The reality of law enforcement is grounded in duty, service, and sacrifice. Officers navigate a complex world, where the weight of split-second decisions can mean the difference between life and death. These decisions are made within the framework of the law, with the awareness that each action taken in the line of duty reverberates through the lives of individuals and the community.

The portrayal of police officers in films like Training Day casts a shadow on the public perception of law enforcement, presenting a distorted image that often does not reflect reality. While the character portrayed by Denzel Washington captivates audiences with his antihero charm, it is a portrayal far removed from the truth of policing. Officers are professionals who daily encounter the raw edges of human existence, the pain, the cruelty, and suffering. Yet, they are expected to rise above it, maintaining their composure and humanity.

The relentless exposure to trauma that police officers face is unparalleled in its intensity and constancy. It is a testament to their resilience that they continue to serve, often with a smile, a kind word, and an unwavering commitment to their communities. They stand as the line between order and chaos, not as avengers, but as steadfast protectors, as public servants who perform their roles with an acute awareness of the trust placed in them by the public they serve.

Few individuals are exposed to such ongoing trauma as police officers. Yet, they are expected to keep a smile, act professionally, and make those split-second decisions mistake-free.

The average police officer experiences 188 critical incidents during their career.[95] This number dwarfs the number of critical incidents experienced by the average person. Unsurprisingly, this trauma and ongoing stress lead to various lousy life outcomes for officers, including obesity, cardiovascular disease, sleeplessness, cancer, and suicide.[96] Police officers suffer from higher rates of divorce and alcohol issues as well.

In recognition of the challenges law enforcement faces, it is incumbent upon society to understand the stark difference between the fictional narratives of cinema and the real-world responsibilities of police officers.

---

[95] "Crime and Community Policing in 2023: Challenges and Strategies," International Public Safety Association, accessed June 3, 2023, https://www.joinipsa.org/IPSA-Blog/7334025.

[96] "On-the-Job Stress Negatively Impacts Police Officer Health, Study Suggests," EHS Today, accessed June 3, 2023, https://www.ehstoday.com/health/article/21915261/onthejob-stress-negatively-impacts-police-officer-health-study-suggests#:~:text=The%20findings%20reveal%20that%20police,%2C%20suicide%2C%20sleeplessness%20and%20cancer.

They are human, fallible, and capable of error, but their role is not to mete out personal justice.

Instead, their mission is to ensure that justice, as defined by our laws and courts, is upheld, that the process is respected and that the rights of all individuals, victims and suspects alike, are protected. It is a noble, demanding, and often thankless task that is essential to maintaining order, the protection of our rights, and the cornerstone of our civil society.

A discussion about the police not usurping the judiciary's authority must include a conversation about police use of force.

The use of force by police officers is one of the most critical and scrutinized aspects of law enforcement, a subject that sits heavily in the public consciousness and ignites debates across the nation. When an officer wields the power to restrict a person's freedom or to exert deadly force, they wield a power that has immediate and profound effects, potentially circumventing the judiciary process.

The imperative for law enforcement to *"get it right"* cannot be overstated—each action taken in the line of duty is a testament to their training, judgment, and the trust society places in them. It's not just the mechanics of handling a weapon drilled into officers during their extensive firearms training; it's the weighty decision of when to use it, where the moral and ethical considerations are as critical as the physical skill.

While officers are trained to aim for center mass—aiming not to kill but to neutralize a threat—the stark reality of a gunfight often reveals the chasm between training and the chaotic nature of real-world confrontations. The statistics on police firearm accuracy in such high-stress scenarios are sobering. An examination by the New York Police Department of their officers' hit rates over eight years highlighted this disconnect; officers involved in gunfights only struck their intended targets at an average rate of 18 percent.[97] These figures lay bare the complexity and unpredictability of such dire situations.

In 2005, for example, NYPD officers fired their guns 472 times in a gunfight and only hit their mark 82 times, for a hit rate of only 17.4 percent.

---

[97] "Trained officers have a 18 percent hit rate, yet we want to arm teachers?" Atlanta Journal-Constitution, accessed June 3, 2023, https://www.ajc.com/blog/get-schooled/gunfights-trained-officers-have-percent-hit-rate-yet-want-arm-teachers/mDBlhDtV6Na4wJVpeu58cM/.

Despite these numbers, some believe police officers should only shoot to injure or wound.[98] In theory, shooting to injure someone sounds like an excellent idea. But in reality, doing so is a tricky proposition.

In the ongoing quest to enhance policing tactics and uphold public safety, the LaGrange Police Department, under the stewardship of Chief Lou Dekmar, embarked on a pioneering approach in 2021. The department introduced a Shoot to Incapacitate program, charting new territory in the use of force by officers.[99] This initiative emerged in response to complex scenarios where officers might face armed individuals whose weapons are not firearms, yet the situation legally justifies the use of deadly force.

The program's essence is a nuanced shift from the conventional doctrine of shooting at center mass—a method traditionally taught to law enforcement officers to ensure the highest likelihood of neutralizing a lethal threat. Instead, officers in LaGrange are trained to aim at areas of the body that would incapacitate but are less likely to be fatal, thereby potentially preserving life while still addressing the immediate threat.

This Shoot to Incapacitate policy is not without its debates and challenges. It requires officers to make split-second decisions with even greater precision under stress, a task that is already profoundly demanding. The policy acknowledges the grave responsibility of discharging a weapon and seeks to balance the imperative of stopping a threat with the sanctity of human life.

Although some law enforcement leaders view the LaGrange PD shoot to incapacitate policy as progressive and thinking outside the box, other leaders view the policy skeptically.

As law enforcement agencies nationwide scrutinize their use-of-force policies, LaGrange's program could offer an alternative that aligns more closely with community expectations and the ethical use of force. It represents a commitment to innovative and compassionate policing, where

---

[98] "Midkiff: Police are not judge, jury or executioner," Columbia Missourian, accessed June 3, 2023, https://www.columbiamissourian.com/midkiff-police-are-not-judge-jury-or-executioner/article_08cedc3a-57c6-11e8-a74f-6ff64d6f7075.html.

[99] "In Georgia, agency: Police train to shoot, not kill," Atlanta Journal-Constitution, accessed June 3, 2023, https://www.ajc.com/news/crime/in-georgia-agency-police-train-to-shoot-not-kill/IJNVJCHXBRHJHKPFHLEXQ672YI/.

the objective is to protect the public from harm and minimize the loss of life wherever possible.

Implementing such a program necessitates rigorous training and a cultural shift within the department, which stresses the importance of restraint, precision, and a deep understanding of the consequences of each bullet discharged. This approach could serve as a model for other departments seeking to reform their use-of-force policies, contributing to a broader conversation about law enforcement's role and responsibilities in society.

In LaGrange, the Shoot to Incapacitate initiative is a testament to the evolution of policing practices. It reflects the department's dedication to aligning its actions with community values and the ethical imperatives of modern law enforcement.

Only time will tell if the policy has its desired effect, but it certainly holds promise.

When discussing the impact of law enforcement actions, it's crucial to consider the number of fatal encounters to the total number of arrests and interactions police have with the public. The figure provided by the Washington Post – approximately 1,000 people killed by police officers annually – is indeed a serious and sobering statistic that calls for reflection and, where necessary, reform.[100] However, this figure should also be contextualized within the broader scope of law enforcement activities, which include 10 million arrests and 61 million police-citizen encounters each year.

The stark contrast between the number of fatalities and the much larger number of police interactions suggests that the vast majority of these interactions do not result in lethal outcomes. This is an essential point in the discussion about police use of force and society's perception of law enforcement. It implies that while any loss of life is tragic and the use of lethal force must always be closely scrutinized and regulated, these instances are relatively rare in the grand scheme of police work.

In light of these statistics, law enforcement agencies must continue refining their training programs, emphasizing de-escalation, crisis management, and community policing. This is not to minimize the significance of the fatalities but to acknowledge that comprehensive training can help

---

[100] "Contacts Between Police and the Public, 2018 - Statistical Tables," Office of Justice Programs, accessed June 3, 2023, https://www.ojp.gov/library/publications/contacts-between-police-and-public-2018-statistical-tables.

reduce these incidents even further. Moreover, each incident must be investigated thoroughly to ensure accountability and to learn lessons that can inform future training and policies.

While the numbers provided give a quantitative perspective, it is also vital to consider the qualitative aspects of each incident, as each case profoundly impacts the individuals involved and the community at large. It reminds us of the need for careful, compassionate, and just policing that respects the dignity and rights of all individuals.

In over 99 percent of arrests or police-citizens encounters, deadly force is not used, which is a significant statistic that gets lost in the discussion about police use of force.

The rarity of a police officer's use of force reflects on their extensive training in conflict resolution, de-escalation techniques, and a commitment to preserving life. It speaks to the professional standards upheld by most police officers who navigate complex and potentially dangerous situations daily. Their primary tools are communication, patience, and a deep understanding of human behavior, leaning on force only as a last resort when all other options have failed or are not viable due to the immediate risk.

This context is significant because it suggests that policing, at its core, is not antagonistic to the community's welfare. Instead, it is inherently protective, seeking to resolve conflicts with the minimum force necessary. It highlights the importance of continued investments in training, community policing initiatives, and mental health resources, which can further reduce the need for force.

Understanding the broader picture painted by these statistics can foster a more nuanced public conversation about law enforcement. It allows for a recognition of the challenges police officers face and the complex decisions they must make, often under life-threatening circumstances. It also reinforces the need for ongoing dialogue, transparency, and accountability within law enforcement agencies to maintain and enhance the trust of the communities they serve.

In this broader narrative, it's essential to balance the recognition of policing's complexities with a commitment to continuous improvement. Acknowledging the low incidence of force is not a dismissal of the instances where things have gone wrong but a call to understand them in context and seek solutions that support officer safety and community trust.

In law enforcement, extensive training and policy development are crucial in ensuring that the use of lethal force is minimized. Modern policing strategies are committed to the sanctity of life, emphasizing de-escalation tactics, crisis intervention, and awareness of implicit biases. Officers are taught to resort to force only when there is no viable alternative and, even then, to use it judiciously.

Introducing technology like body-worn and dashboard cameras has revolutionized transparency and accountability in police operations. These devices serve as objective witnesses to police-citizen encounters, providing a clear record that can be reviewed to confirm the appropriateness of an officer's response or to initiate corrective measures when necessary.

While the use of deadly force by police is a matter of grave concern and demands scrutiny, it is but a small fraction of the totality of police work. Each incident and statistic is a life, a story, and must be treated with the utmost seriousness. It is the responsibility of law enforcement agencies to constantly refine their practices, ensuring they not only follow but also set the highest standards of public safety and justice.

Public attention tends to focus on the rare instances of lethal force, but it is essential to recognize the broader context of law enforcement. Most police-citizen interactions are resolved without force, a testament to the effectiveness of current training and policies. However, this does not diminish the importance of each life affected by police action nor the work that remains to be done.

Yet, law enforcement is frequently attacked for being a judge, jury, and executioner.[101] A quick search of *"police as judge, jury and executioner"* in Google returned 771,000 results.

Also, former NYPD detective Frank Serpico, famous for exposing corruption in the NYPD in the 1970s, spoke out against police being judge, jury, and executioner.[102] Serpico said, *"Police fail to grasp that they are*

---

[101]   "Ilhan Omar Says Police Can't Be 'Judge, Jury, Executioner' Following Rayshard Brooks Shooting Death," Newsweek, accessed June 3, 2023, https://www.newsweek.com/ilhan-omar-says-police-cant-judge-jury-executioner-following-rayshard-brooks-shooting-death-1510778.

[102]   John W. Whitehead, "The Machinery of Death: When Government Acts as Judge, Jury, and Executioner," LinkedIn, accessed June 3, 2023, https://www.linkedin.com/pulse/machinery-death-when-government-acts-judge-jury-john-whitehead/?trackingId=GBs%2F%2FzdA9MZ7I8zTe7rAsQ%3D%3D.

public servants for peace. They should provide a civil service to enforce the laws equally, without bias, and with discretion. They must understand that they do not have immunity or special privileges and — most importantly — are just responsible for apprehending suspects, and should not act as judge, jury, and executioner, which too many of them truly believe themselves to be."

The difference between public perception and the realities of law enforcement is a conundrum that the digital age has magnified. The use of force by police, though statistically rare in the vast sea of police-citizen interactions, has a profound impact on public trust. Each negative outcome feeds into the narrative that police overstep their bounds, acting as judge, jury, and executioner. Sir Robert Peel's principles, which emphasize the police's role in preventing crime without repressive force, seem at odds with such outcomes. Certainly, Frank Serpico's insights into police integrity resonate with this timeless ideal.

The ubiquity of video footage and the virality of social media content have indeed shaped public discourse on police conduct. These platforms, while influential in highlighting issues of concern, can also amplify isolated incidents, sometimes skewing public perception and overshadowing the countless positive police-citizen interactions that occur daily.

There is a broad consensus among law enforcement leaders on the necessity of accountability, especially when officers' actions might circumvent the judiciary's due process. It is rare to find a police executive who would contest the importance of such accountability. However, opinions on how to address these issues can be extreme and varied.

Take, for instance, the pundit from Missouri who suggests that legislation should prohibit police from using deadly force even when they perceive a threat.[103] This viewpoint, while certainly on the fringes, highlights the complexity and contentiousness of the debate on the use-of-force policies.

In navigating these challenges, law enforcement agencies must balance the need for officer safety with the public's call for restraint and

---

[103] Ken Midkiff, "Ken Midkiff: In Missouri, police officers should not be allowed to make life-or-death decisions," Columbia Missourian, accessed June 3, 2023, https://www.columbiamissourian.com/opinion/local_columnists/ken-midkiff-in-missouri-police-officers-should-not-be-allowed/article_c92b9dc2-5165-11e8-a351-4b3789ca2cc1.html.

judicious use of force. Training in de-escalation, crisis intervention, and community engagement becomes beneficial and essential.

Moreover, fostering a culture of transparency and communication can demystify police work, allowing the public to gain a more significant understanding of the challenges officers face and the processes in place to ensure justice and fairness.

Building and maintaining public trust in law enforcement ultimately hinges on a delicate balance of authority, compassion, and accountability. As law enforcement continues to evolve, Peel's principles remain a guiding light, reminding us that the power to enforce the law comes with the responsibility to uphold the rights and dignity of all individuals.

Accountability in policing is a multifaceted endeavor, crucial to maintaining public trust and ensuring that law enforcement agencies operate within the bounds of law and ethics.

Technological tools, such as body-worn cameras have become critical in promoting transparency and accountability. The presence of cameras acts as an objective observer in police-citizen encounters, often leading to a decline in the use of force and a reduction in complaints against officers.[104]

Other studies dispute and contradict these findings.[105]

However, these devices provide a clear record that can be used to evaluate conduct, train officers, and, if necessary, serve as evidence in disciplinary or legal proceedings.

While not a panacea, body-worn cameras offer a window into the complex and often split-second decisions that officers must make. They also serve as a deterrent to potential misconduct. They can help de-escalate volatile situations, with citizens and officers alike being more mindful of their behavior when aware that an encounter is being recorded.

---

[104] "FY 2014 Comprehensive School Safety Initiative (CSSI) Project Abstracts," Office of Justice Programs, accessed June 3, 2023, https://www.ojp.gov/pdffiles1/nij/grants/251416.pdf.

[105] "Body Cameras May Not Be the Easy Answer Everyone Was Looking For," Pew Trusts, accessed June 3, 2023, https://www.pewtrusts.org/en/research-and-analysis/blogs/stateline/2020/01/14/body-cameras-may-not-be-the-easy-answer-everyone-was-looking-for#:~:text=The%20study%2C%20which%20looked%20at,or%20citizens'%20views%20of%20police.

The integration of body-worn cameras into modern policing has been one of the most significant advancements in law enforcement accountability and transparency. While these cameras are indispensable tools, they are not without their limitations, and understanding these is key to interpreting footage accurately and fairly.

A camera mounted on an officer's uniform provides an objective perspective of an encounter, but it's crucial to recognize that this is not an omniscient view. The camera captures a fixed angle, which may not always align with the officer's gaze. An officer may be responding to a peripheral threat or a subtle movement not apparent in the video. This can create discrepancies between what the camera records and what the officer perceives.[106]

Moreover, cameras cannot fully capture the tactile cues that an officer may detect, such as the tension of a person's body that suggests potential resistance or aggression. These nuances of human behavior and non-verbal communication are often vital to understanding an officer's response to a situation.

Low-light environments pose additional challenges. Body-worn cameras might either enhance or fail to capture details that an officer's eyes cannot see in dim conditions. This can lead to misunderstandings when reviewing footage, as it may present a clearer or more obscured scene than what the officer experienced.

Thus, while body-worn cameras are powerful tools for accountability, they are not a substitute for the complex, multi-sensory process of human perception. It is essential for those reviewing body camera footage to consider these limitations and avoid drawing conclusions based solely on the video without context. Additional evidence, including officer and witness testimonies, physical evidence, and other investigative findings, must also be weighed to comprehensively understand the events in question.

The limitations of body-worn cameras serve as a reminder of the importance of comprehensive policies and training on their use. Police officers must be trained in the mechanical operation of these devices and the policies governing their use, including when to activate them, how

---

[106] "10 Limitations of Body Cams You Need to Know for Your Protection," Force Science Institute, accessed June 3, 2023, https://www.forcescience.com/2014/10/10-limitations-of-body-cams-you-need-to-know-for-your-protection/.

to ensure proper maintenance, and the procedures for handling the data captured. Public education on the capabilities and limitations of body-worn cameras is also essential to set realistic expectations about what these devices can and cannot do.

Ultimately, body-worn cameras are a piece of the broader puzzle of policing and public safety. They serve as a crucial check and balance, providing an essential layer of transparency that benefits the community and law enforcement officers. Yet, like any tool, they are most effective as part of a holistic approach to fair and just policing.

Despite these shortcomings, having a body-worn camera recording during a critical incident can be the difference between a general acceptance of the details of an incident rather than open skepticism.

The deployment of body-worn cameras in modern policing has become critical in fostering public trust and providing a transparent account of officers' actions, particularly during critical incidents. The objective evidence these cameras provide can be the linchpin in validating the sequence of events as recounted by law enforcement, especially when the facts are under dispute.

Take, for instance, the January 19, 2023, incident involving the Georgia State Patrol. Troopers were tasked with dispersing protesters from a construction site slated for the new Atlanta Police Department training facility. During this operation, a tragic decision by a protester to open fire on a Trooper resulted in the trooper returning fire and fatally wounding the assailant.[107]

In this case, the absence of body-worn camera footage opened the door for critics to question the facts. Without the video and audio record, the troopers' accounts lacked the corroborative evidence that such footage could have provided, opening the door to public skepticism and questions among the family and associates of the deceased. This gap in documentation illustrates the tangible benefits body-worn cameras offer, not just in affirming law enforcement actions but in preserving the public's faith in the investigative process.

---

[107] "GBI: No bodycam footage of Atlanta police training center shooting," Police1, accessed June 3, 2023, https://www.police1.com/officer-shootings/articles/gbi-no-bodycam-footage-of-atlanta-police-training-center-shooting-FM5Ggf4bX-3cohR6p/.

Body-worn cameras serve as unbiased observers, capturing events as they unfold, free from the perception of bias or error that can cloud human recollection. They provide a narrative that can corroborate testimonies, clarify actions taken by officers, and dispel unfounded claims. In many cases, this footage has been instrumental in exonerating officers from unfounded accusations or highlighting misconduct that might otherwise have gone unaddressed.

The call for widespread implementation of body-worn cameras reflects the community's desire for transparency and accountability from its law enforcement agencies. While the initial investment and ongoing management of this technology can be substantial, the value it adds to public trust and the integrity of the justice process is immeasurable.

In the wake of incidents such as the shooting during the protest in Atlanta, the absence of video evidence from body-worn cameras becomes a reminder of the need for such tools. It helps to advance the ongoing discussion among law enforcement agencies, policymakers, and the public about the necessity and value of body-worn cameras as standard equipment for all police operations. The objective is clear: to ensure that truth prevails and justice is served with the utmost transparency and trust.

The actions taken by police departments when officers violate policies are another barometer of their commitment to integrity, justice, and accountability. As such, law enforcement leaders must address even minor policy infractions promptly, as this can prevent more significant issues from arising.

This principle of accountability is particularly crucial when it comes to the use of force. Any deviation from established protocols not only undermines the public's confidence in the police but also raises questions about the fairness of the justice system. When officers act outside the law, the consequences must be unequivocal: termination and, if warranted, prosecution. There should be no ambiguity about the repercussions of such actions.

The stance on truthfulness is equally non-negotiable. Truth is the foundation upon which the credibility of law enforcement rests. If an officer is found to have lied, the typical response from most police chiefs is immediate termination. The message is clear: integrity is a must, and those who breach this trust cannot continue to serve in a role that demands honesty.

However, the issue's complexity is highlighted by the experiences shared among police chiefs. For instance, a respected police commissioner from a large police department, at a national meeting, spoke about his new policy of firing officers who lie, which sparked surprise amongst some police chiefs in the room. This reaction pointed to a disparity in how different departments handle dishonesty within their ranks.

Compounding this challenge is the role of police unions and the arbitration process. While unions play a vital role in protecting the rights of police officers, the reinstatement of officers dismissed for serious violations or criminal behavior is a contentious topic. The arbitration process can sometimes overturn decisions made by police chiefs, leading to the reinstatement of officers whose actions have seriously breached departmental policies or the law.[108]

Ironically, in states that do not have unions or arbitration, police officers who commit acts like many of those reinstated through arbitration stay fired.

This dynamic poses a significant obstacle to proper accountability. Restoring officers who have committed serious offenses can erode public confidence and damage the police force's reputation.

A balanced approach that protects officers' rights while ensuring that those who fail to uphold the law are not permitted to return to positions of authority and trust is needed.

To address these complex issues, an ongoing dialogue among law enforcement leaders, community stakeholders, and policymakers is necessary. Striking the right balance between due process for officers and ensuring accountability is crucial for the credibility and effectiveness of law enforcement agencies. Only through such efforts can police departments maintain the high standards expected by their communities and ensure that those who wear the badge do so with honor and integrity.

We have discussed a police officer's responsibility when it comes to accountability, but what about the obligation of citizens?

In the daily dance between police officers and society, law enforcement and citizenry roles are clearly delineated yet intrinsically linked. Police

---

[108] "How Police Unions Keep Abusive Cops on the Street," The Atlantic, accessed June 3, 2023, https://www.theatlantic.com/politics/archive/2014/12/how-police-unions-keep-abusive-cops-on-the-street/383258/.

officers stand on the frontline of community protection as the upholders of law and order. Citizens, for their part, bear a civic duty to cooperate with these guardians of peace. It is a mutual contract of trust and respect that, when honored, preserves the safety and order of the public realm.

Compliance with law enforcement is not a mere capitulation to authority but a commitment to public safety. Officers trained to navigate the unpredictable currents of societal interactions depend on this coopera-tion to maintain order. When citizens heed the instructions of law enforce-ment, they do not just facilitate the resolution of immediate incidents; they uphold the collective security of their community.

It is a common misconception that compliance might infringe upon individual rights, fostering a reluctance to acquiesce to law enforcement directives. Yet, true compliance is a temporary alliance forged in the pur-suit of safety, not a forfeiture of rights. It allows for the smooth execution of police duties while preserving the individual's right to later address and challenge any perceived injustices fairly and legally.

When the public responds to law enforcement directives, they do so not out of fear or submission but from an understanding of the neces-sity of order and the swift execution of justice. Such collaboration reduces misunderstandings and potential conflicts, allowing officers to perform their responsibilities effectively and without undue risk to themselves or the public.

Historically, law enforcement has not collected data on police use of force nationally. Instead, various advocacy and media groups have attempted to create different police use of force databases.

For example, the Washington Post has collected data on police shootings since 2015, primarily relying on media reports to compile their data.[109] At best, this database and others like it are incomplete. At worst, they have a preconceived view of police use of force and present a biased point of view.

---

[109] "Fatal Force: 2015 Police Shootings Database," The Washington Post, accessed June 3, 2023, https://www.washingtonpost.com/graphics/investigations/police-shootings-database/.

Approximately 21 states require some form of data collection on police use of force from law enforcement agencies in their state.[110] The data collection type and reporting requirements vary from state to state.

Navigating the maze of use-of-force data across the United States presents a significant challenge due to the variance in state reporting requirements. This disparity hampers the ability to draw national comparisons and to holistically understand the patterns and practices of police use of force. It's a puzzle where pieces are shaped by local mandates, making the complete picture elusive.

The quest for a centralized and comprehensive national database of police use-of-force incidents has long been recognized as a pivotal step toward greater transparency and accountability. In 2015, the Federal Bureau of Investigation (FBI) laid the groundwork for such an endeavor with the inception of the National Use-of-Force Data Collection program. With a pilot phase launched in 2017, this program marked a concerted effort to gather detailed information on a national scale.

As the chief of the Dunwoody Police Department, my participation in the pilot was a testament to our commitment to this cause. By 2019, the program expanded nationally, yet the landscape of participation remained patchy—with only 40 percent of law enforcement agencies reporting their data. This reluctance highlights a collective hesitance within the law enforcement community to participate. This hesitance risks undermining the very foundation of trust and credibility we strive to build with the public we serve.

The reality is that voluntary participation may not suffice in the quest for a comprehensive dataset. The inevitability of mandatory reporting looms on the horizon, a mandate that could serve as the impetus for a richer, more valuable compilation of use-of-force statistics. Such mandatory reporting would standardize data collection and pave the way for more informed policy-making, training programs, and community relations strategies.

A mandatory national database could offer the clarity and insights necessary to foster trust and inform dialogue in a society yearning for a

---

[110] "Use of Force Data Collection," National Conference of State Legislatures, accessed June 3, 2023, https://www.ncsl.org/research/civil-and-criminal-justice/use-of-force-data.aspx.

deeper understanding of law enforcement practices. As law enforcement leaders, it is incumbent upon us to embrace this transparency, recognizing that an accurate analysis of police use of force, free from the confines of regional reporting discrepancies, is not only beneficial but essential for the evolution of policing in America.

The architectural wisdom of our Founding Fathers is reflected in the three-branch system of government, a testament to the foresight that each branch should have a distinct and independent role. The delineation is clear: the legislature crafts laws, the judiciary interprets them, and law enforcement, as part of the executive branch, implements them. This separation of powers is a cornerstone of our democracy, ensuring a balance that prevents the concentration of power and the abuse that might ensue.

Sir Robert Peel grasped the perils that could arise from an overlap of these functions. He understood that for society to flourish under the rule of law, trust in law enforcement institutions must be absolute. Peel envisioned a policing system where officers were guardians of peace rather than arbiters of punishment, a vision reverberating into our modern societal fabric through the ages.

Yet, the landscape of trust is uneven, marred by instances where it has frayed at the edges. Restoring trust where it has waned is not just an aspiration; it's a necessity. Trust is the bedrock upon which effective policing is built, without which societal structure is weakened. It is the currency of policing, and when it is in deficit, the legitimacy of law enforcement is called into question.

If law enforcement fails to regulate itself, legislative mandates will fill the vacuum. These laws will be shaped by the collective will of a society yearning for reform, for a guarantee that the police serve with integrity and accountability. It is imperative, therefore, that the police not only enforce the law but do so with a commitment to the principles of justice and equality that Peel so ardently espoused.

In this endeavor, the police must not stand alone. It is a collective journey that requires the engagement of all stakeholders—law enforcement, the community, and the government. Together, they can navigate the complex terrain of modern policing, ensuring that the ideals Peel set forth nearly two centuries ago remain relevant.

Peel's Principles in Practice: Questions for Today's Challenges and Opportunities

Police Officers

1. In what ways does your department engage with CALEA or state certification processes to ensure you are meeting professional standards?
2. What are your department's policies regarding the use of force, and how do they compare to the best practices recognized by CALEA and your state?
3. How does your department collect and utilize community feedback during the CALEA accreditation or state certification process?
4. What training and resources are provided to your department's officers to help manage the ongoing trauma and stress associated with your duties?
5. What systems are in place for accountability when policies are violated, particularly regarding use-of-force incidents?

Citizens

1. How does your local police department align with the three-branch structure of government to maintain a balance of power and protect individual rights?
2. Is your department CALEA Accredited or State Certified?
3. What is your local police department's policy regarding the use of force, and how does it compare to national standards or community expectations?
4. How does your police department ensure that it does not overstep its authority and respects the role of the judiciary in the criminal justice system?
5. How does your police department support its officers in dealing with the high levels of stress and trauma associated with their duties?
6. Does your local police department contribute data to the National Use of Force Data Collection program? If not, why not?
7. Does your local police department have a Peer Support program for officers?

PRINCIPLE #9

*To recognise always that the **test** of police efficiency is the **absence** of crime and disorder, and not the visible evidence of police **action** in dealing with them.*

Measuring a police department's performance is indeed a complex endeavor that extends well beyond the simplicity of crime statistics. Sir Robert Peel's notion that the absence of crime and disorder is the ultimate measure of effective policing serves as an aspirational goal.

However, the modern approach recognizes many interwoven factors that influence both crime rates and the perceptions of safety and order within a community.

The multifaceted nature of crime and its precipitators calls for a nuanced understanding. The Federal Bureau of Investigation has identified various variables affecting crime levels. Population density and urbanization can impact the nature and number of offenses, with densely populated urban areas often presenting different challenges than rural communities.

Demographic factors like age and gender distribution also play a role, as they correlate with certain types of criminal behavior.[111]

Socioeconomic conditions are particularly influential. High levels of poverty, limited job opportunities, and low median incomes are often associated with higher crime rates. In contrast, factors such as widespread access to quality education and stable family environments can serve as buffers against the inclination to engage in criminal activities.

The physical and social environment, including modes of transportation and climate, can also affect how and when crimes are committed. A robust public transit system, for example, may both aid in the mobility of a city's residents and create potential opportunities for certain types of crimes.

Of course, this is not an exhaustive list. Instead, it is evidence that reducing crime is a more complicated proposition than first evident.

To effectively assess a police department's performance, it is essential to consider these factors and more. Metrics such as crime rates, clearance rates, and response times are commonly used. Yet, equally important is the public's trust and confidence in their law enforcement agencies, which can be gauged through surveys and community feedback mechanisms.

Moreover, the adoption of community policing practices, the degree of transparency and accountability, the quality of police-citizen interactions, and the department's ability to adapt to changing circumstances are all critical barometers of performance. A department that fosters positive relationships with the community engages in problem-solving strategies, and works collaboratively with citizens to address the root causes of crime and disorder will likely be viewed as successful.

Reflecting on my tenure in law enforcement, I can attest that there have been years where, despite every concerted effort, crime rates have edged upwards. Conversely, there have been times when crime has decreased, even though our approach hadn't markedly changed from the previous year. This oscillation serves as a humbling reminder that crime trends are subject to various factors, some of which are beyond the control of the police.

While undeniable, law enforcement's influence on crime rates must be contextualized within a broader societal framework. Police leaders must, therefore, navigate the delicate balance between claiming credit for

---

[111] "Variables Affecting Crime," FBI, accessed June 3, 2023, https://ucr.fbi.gov/nibrs/2012/resources/variables-affecting-crime.

crime reductions and accepting accountability for increases. A myriad of elements contribute to crime dynamics.

That said, the role of strategic policing cannot be overlooked. Bill Bratton introduced Broken Windows Policing to New York's transit system in the early 1990s when he was chief of the New York Transit Police and experienced great results.[112]

As Commissioner of the New York Police Department, Bill Bratton oversaw the implementation of the CompStat program, which exemplifies a proactive and data-centric approach to law enforcement associated with notable successes in crime reduction. Introduced in 1994, CompStat revolutionized police work by integrating four pivotal principles: the timely and accurate collection of data, rapid deployment of resources, employment of effective tactics, and rigorous follow-up and assessment.[113]

The program's cornerstone lies in its ability to provide a real-time snapshot of crime, allowing the NYPD to allocate resources dynamically and respond to emerging trends with agility. Through consistent evaluation and adaptation of tactics, the department has fostered a culture of continuous improvement and accountability.

Moreover, CompStat's focus on follow-up ensures that strategies are implemented and evaluated for effectiveness, with adjustments made as needed. This iterative process has proven to be instrumental in the NYPD's ability to address crime proactively and instill a sense of urgency and responsibility at all department levels.

The results speak for themselves. By 1998, homicides dropped by 67 percent, burglary was down 53 percent, and robberies were down 54 percent.[114] This decline in crime continued for many years, reaching historic lows for homicides.

---

[112] Cape Cod Times, "William Bratton's Book 'The Profession' Notes Police Faults, Offers Solutions," August 25, 2021, accessed May 31, 2023, https://www.capecodtimes.com/story/news/2021/08/25/william-bratton-book-the-profession-notes-police-faults-offers-solutions/8201394002/.

[113] Police Executive Research Forum, "PERF and Compstat: A Process Evaluation" (Washington, D.C.: Bureau of Justice Assistance, Office of Justice Programs, U.S. Department of Justice, n.d.), accessed June 3, 2023, https://bja.ojp.gov/sites/g/files/xyckuh186/files/Publications/PERF-Compstat.pdf.

[114] Ibid

Despite what appears to be a great success, some detractors suggest CompStat's reliance on numbers created a monster. They point to the stop, question, and frisk of hundreds of thousands of brown and black New Yorkers.[115]

Others, including Eli Silverman and John Eterno (a retired captain with NYPD), suggest that the push for arrests and results led to abusive police practices, unnecessary and counterproductive over-policing, and even police commanders falsifying their crime numbers to make themselves look better.[116] Silverman and Eterno documented these concerns in their book, The Crime Numbers Game.

Still, CompStat grew in popularity and spread to other police agencies across the United States.

The Marietta Police Department's implementation of the M-STAR program in 1998, during my tenure, marked a significant transition towards data-driven policing in our community. Mirroring the principles of the New York Police Department's CompStat program, M-STAR stands for Marietta Strategically Targeting Areas with Resources. The program's introduction correlated with a marked decline in crime over the next decade, marking the value of such targeted approaches.

The success of M-STAR in Marietta was not an isolated phenomenon. Police departments across the United States began adopting similar data-focused strategies, tailoring the CompStat model to their unique community needs and challenges. This nationwide shift towards strategic, analytical approaches in policing was not merely a trend but a fundamental evolution in crime prevention and law enforcement.

A comprehensive study by the Brennan Center for Justice at New York University's School of Law in 2015 offered empirical support for the positive impact of these programs. The findings indicated that

---

[115] Christopher Beam, "The Crime-Fighting Program That Changed New York Forever," New York Magazine, March 5, 2018, accessed June 3, 2023, https://nymag.com/intelligencer/2018/03/the-crime-fighting-program-that-changed-new-york-forever.html.

[116] Timothy Williams, "CompStat: How computer analysis became integral to modern policing," USA Today, February 9, 2017, accessed June 3, 2023, https://www.usatoday.com/story/opinion/policing/spotlight/2017/02/09/compstat-computer-police-policing-the-usa-community/97568874/.

CompStat-style programs contributed to a significant reduction in crime across the board — with a 13 percent decrease in violent crime, an 11 percent decrease in property crime, and a 13 percent decrease in homicides nationally.[117]

These statistics testify to the power of combining traditional policing with modern analytics and strategic resource allocation. By focusing on hotspots, identifying patterns, and deploying resources where they are most needed, law enforcement agencies can react more effectively to crime and preempt and prevent it.

The implications of these findings are profound. They suggest that when police departments can analyze crime data in real time, adjust their tactics accordingly, and maintain a relentless focus on results, they can make significant strides in safeguarding their communities. Moreover, such strategies enhance the overall efficiency of police work, allowing departments to do more with their available resources.

Although the true impact of CompStat on the crime rate may be disputed, the fact that CompStat revolutionized the way police departments attack crime is not.

As we continue to refine and innovate within law enforcement, the lessons learned from CompStat and its derivatives remain clear: informed, agile, and responsive policing is crucial to reducing crime and enhancing public safety. These approaches should be part of any forward-thinking law enforcement strategy, not only as a means to suppress crime but also as a way to strengthen community trust and cooperation. Pursuing such strategic initiatives, grounded in Peel's core principles, will be essential as we navigate the evolving landscape of public safety in the coming years.

The introduction of CompStat heralded a revolutionary shift in policing strategy, emphasizing data-driven tactics to address crime. Yet, as with any significant change, there have been unintended consequences, such as the perception of an "*unofficial*" quota system. The pressure to meet statistical benchmarks for stops, citations, and arrests can lead to an unhealthy emphasis on quantity over quality in law enforcement actions.

---

[117]   Rutrell Yasin, "Compstat 2.0: New Reporting Tool Changes Policing," GCN, March 17, 2015, accessed June 3, 2023, https://gcn.com/Articles/2015/03/17/Compstat-report.aspx?m=1.

Reflecting on the early days of my career, the emphasis on metrics was evident. Monthly tallies of each officer's arrests and citations were common, emphasizing a numbers-driven approach. While it's true that officers should be accountable for their time on duty, a quota system is an antiquated solution that has led to numerous challenges and criticisms.

The New York Police Department, due to its size and influence, has often been at the center of this debate. It's not the only department to grapple with such issues, but its high profile has meant that its challenges with quota systems have been well-documented and scrutinized. Historical instances, such as a 1957 lawsuit over a department-wide traffic summons quota and a 1972 incident where a commander's summons quota led to over a thousand parking tickets in a single day, highlight the problematic nature of these systems.[118]

The Knapp Commission blamed narcotic and gambling unit quotas on police corruption and prevented officers from addressing these critical issues.[119]

In 2008, NYPD Officer Polanco secretly recorded his Sergeant speaking about a requirement to issue 20 citations and have one arrest per month. The sergeant suggested that the number could rise to 25 and one or 35 and one in the future. Officer Polanco eventually filed a lawsuit as a whistleblower to expose this practice.[120]

In New York today, it is illegal for an employer to *"transfer or in any other manner penalize or threaten, expressly or impliedly"* a police officer *"based in whole or in part on such employee's failure to meet a quota."*[121]

These examples from the NYPD illustrate the potential pitfalls of a quota system, where the drive to meet numerical goals can overshadow

118   Bronstein, Michael V., "Police Misconduct and Public Policy" (2017), Columbia Journal of Law & Social Problems, accessed June 3, 2023, http://jlsp.law.columbia.edu/wp-content/uploads/sites/8/2017/03/48-Bronstein.pdf.

119   Ibid

120   Martin Kaste, "Despite Laws and Lawsuits, Quota-Based Policing Lingers," NPR, April 4, 2015, accessed June 3, 2023, https://www.npr.org/2015/04/04/395061810/despite-laws-and-lawsuits-quota-based-policing-lingers.

121   Bronstein, Michael V. "Police Misconduct and Public Policy" (2017). Columbia Journal of Law & Social Problems. Accessed June 3, 2023. http://jlsp.law.columbia.edu/wp-content/uploads/sites/8/2017/03/48-Bronstein.pdf.

the broader objectives of community safety and justice. Quotas can lead to adverse outcomes, such as strained community relations, perceptions of over-policing, and diminished public trust in law enforcement.

The lessons from these experiences are clear: while productivity and accountability are vital, they must not come at the cost of fairness and the community's well-being. Police departments must seek a balanced approach that values the qualitative aspects of policing—such as community engagement, problem-solving, and prevention—as much as the quantitative. Moving away from a strictly numbers-based assessment towards a more holistic evaluation of police effectiveness can help restore balance and trust in law enforcement.

So, if quotas are prohibited, are viewed as inappropriate, and don't work, how can police departments reduce crime and disorder without the visible action of the police mentioned by Peel?

In the book **Think Again** by Adam Grant, the author suggests that focusing on outcomes can be detrimental to long-term learning and growth. This concept is directly applicable to policing. Officers incentivized to produce high numbers might prioritize arrests and citations over more nuanced and community-oriented approaches. Such a focus might discourage the exploration of alternative solutions that could be more effective in the long run.

Police departments can adopt various strategies to foster a positive impact on crime and disorder without resorting to overt and aggressive tactics.

The essence of impactful policing lies not just in enforcing laws but also in fostering a culture of engagement where police and community members collaborate as partners. This shift from an "*us versus them*" mindset to a unified "*we*" perspective is critical in addressing the root causes of crime and disorder.

Engagement goes beyond mere interaction; it involves police officers building genuine relationships with citizens and community stakeholders, listening to their concerns, and working together towards shared goals. Recognizing and rewarding such engagement is a potent method of promoting this behavior. When officers are commended for their community involvement, whether through formal awards or informal acknowledgment, it sets a positive precedent and encourages others to follow suit.

An engaged community is an informed and proactive one. Citizens who are aware of and invested in the safety and well-being of their neighborhoods are invaluable allies in the fight against crime. Stakeholder engagement is paramount today, especially as communities and law enforcement agencies navigate complex social issues.

Problem-oriented policing (POP) is another powerful strategy that targets the underlying conditions leading to crime. By identifying specific problems and addressing them directly, law enforcement can reduce crime opportunities. This proactive approach requires critical thinking, creativity, and collaboration, often involving stakeholders such as local businesses, community organizations, and other governmental agencies.[122]

Incorporating citizen feedback through surveys is an invaluable strategy for gauging community sentiment toward law enforcement. By conducting biennial surveys, the city of Dunwoody exemplifies a commitment to understanding and evolving with its citizens' perspectives. This practice offers a quantifiable measure of the community's trust and satisfaction, allowing the police department to effectively adapt and improve its services.

The infusion of significant resources into technology, data management, and training demonstrates a police department's commitment to transitioning effectively to data-driven methods. It is essential to democratize these advancements, ensuring that all law enforcement agencies, irrespective of size or budget, have equitable access to the tools and training necessary for effective data-driven policing.

Looking to the future, the potential applications of advanced analytics in policing are vast. Incorporating artificial intelligence and machine learning can refine predictive policing while emerging technologies like video analytics, social media analysis, and IoT devices promise a broader and more nuanced understanding of crime patterns.

Crucially, data-driven policing can act as a conduit for enhanced cooperation between law enforcement entities. Law enforcement agencies can unify their efforts against increasingly sophisticated criminal enterprises by fostering robust data-sharing networks, transcending traditional geographic and jurisdictional limitations.

The transformative impact of data-driven policing extends beyond crime analysis and prevention; it can fundamentally alter the relationship

---

122   "Problem-Oriented Policing," RAND Corporation, accessed June 3, 2023, https://www.rand.org/pubs/tools/TL261/better-policing-toolkit/all-strategies/problem-oriented-policing.html.

between law enforcement and the community. By adopting a transparent, data-informed approach, police departments can build trust, validate their strategies with evidence, and engage in more meaningful community partnerships. This paradigm shift represents a step forward in the evolution of policing, aligning closely with the community-oriented ethos pivotal to maintaining public safety and trust in the 21st century.

In a world where trust in law enforcement is crucial, transparency within police departments has taken center stage. It's the cornerstone of a modern, community-oriented approach to policing that recognizes the importance of public trust and legitimacy.

The very essence of transparency serves as a check against potential abuses of power, encouraging a behavior of self-regulation among officers who are aware that their actions are subject to public view. This level of scrutiny not only deters misconduct but also ensures that, in instances where misconduct does occur, the response is swift, fair, and visible to the public. The result is a reinforced belief in the system's integrity and fairness.

The positive ripple effects of transparency within a police department cannot be overstated. It cultivates a foundation of reciprocal trust between the police and the community. It's an acknowledgment that both parties play a role in maintaining public safety and enforcing the law. By adopting transparency as a guiding principle, police departments can strengthen community relations, encourage cooperation, and promote a safer society.

Ultimately, the drive towards greater transparency is a response to a societal call for law enforcement that is effective but also equitable and accountable. It's a commitment to building a police department that stands as a pillar of its community, fostering an environment where mutual respect and collaboration are the norms and where every individual—officer and civilian alike—contributes to the collective well-being.

Gauging the professional operation of a police department extends far beyond traditional metrics such as crime rates or arrest figures. In his book **How to Rate Your Local Police**, retired Madison Police Chief David Couper challenges conventional wisdom by debunking four myths that often misguide assessments of police performance.

Myth #1 posits that low crime rates are indicative of police efficiency. However, Couper refutes this by suggesting that crime rates are influenced by many factors, with the police's modus operandi being just one. It's a narrow lens that fails to account for the complexities of crime dynamics and ignores the multifaceted roles police departments play in ensuring public safety.

Countering Myth #2, Couper argues that high arrest rates should not be the benchmark of success for police departments. The fundamental goals of law enforcement—crime control, order maintenance, and service provision—aren't accurately reflected in arrest statistics alone. Arrests are a means to an end, not the end itself, and should not overshadow broader objectives.

Myth #3 equates a high police-to-citizen ratio with superior police service, a claim Couper dismisses. Such a ratio doesn't consider each community's unique social and economic fabric, its public service usage patterns, the nature of local crime, or the community's expectations of its police force.

Myth #4 correlates rapid response times to calls for service with efficiency. Couper suggests a more nuanced approach, advocating for a response strategy tailored to the gravity of the call, the timing of the incident, and the specific needs of the caller to provide the most reasonable and effective police service.

In the quest to evaluate a police department's effectiveness, retired Chief David Couper proposes a shift from traditional metrics to a more comprehensive assessment focusing on leadership, policy, and organization. This approach aligns with a deeper understanding of community-oriented policing and recognizes the nuanced realities of law enforcement's role in society. To delve into the organization's quality, Chief Couper provides a set of reflective suggestions to guide an evaluation of your local police department.

1. Respect for individual rights is paramount in policing. Officers must uphold constitutional protections and human dignity in every interaction, ensuring that their conduct remains within the bounds of law and ethical standards.

2. Addressing crime and maintaining order should not fall solely on the police; it requires a collective effort. A competent police agency actively engages with community organizations, leveraging diverse resources to address public safety issues holistically.

3. Cooperation and coordination with neighboring law enforcement and criminal justice entities are essential for cohesive public safety strategies, facilitating a unified approach to crime prevention and investigation.

4. Open lines of communication between the police and the public they serve are vital. Regular and transparent dialogue fosters trust, demystifies policing activities, and enables community feedback.

5. The approach to media relations reflects a department's commitment to transparency. Proactive and constructive engagement with media can help disseminate information effectively, manage crises, and shape public perception.

While Chief Couper offers a valuable framework for scrutinizing police departments, the absence of a universally accepted rating system highlights the complexity of quantifying police performance. The effectiveness of policing is influenced by myriad factors, including but not limited to community relations, policy enforcement, and adaptability to evolving societal needs. As such, any rating system should be dynamic, multifaceted, and sensitive to the local context to provide a fair and accurate representation of a department's performance.

The true measure of a police department's efficiency is rooted in the department's culture, its rapport with the community, and a wide array of intricate factors that interplay within law enforcement. The essence of policing is not captured by quantitative outcomes alone but is deeply embedded in the quality of the connections fostered with those they serve.

Building and sustaining positive relationships with community members represents a more nuanced and challenging aspect of policing that requires an ongoing commitment to understanding, empathy, and engagement. Such relationships are the bedrock of trust and collaboration, leading to safer communities and more effective policing. Simple metrics can't quantify them, but their impact is profound and long-lasting.

Departments that recognize the "*numbers trap*" can avoid the pitfalls of reducing policing to a series of transactions. Instead, they invest in the more complex, more rewarding work of creating a culture of service that values every individual interaction. This approach champions the belief that every encounter is an opportunity to build trust and legitimacy, contributing to the overall mission of public safety and community well-being. This holistic perspective is paramount in evaluating a department's effectiveness and success.

Peel's Principles in Practice: Questions for Today's Challenges and Opportunities

Police Officers

1. How does your department measure success beyond crime statistics?
2. In what ways is your department engaging with different demographics to understand and prevent crime specific to these groups?
3. How does your department encourage quality police-citizen interactions, and how are these evaluated?
4. How is your department leveraging technology and data, like CompStat, to inform your policing tactics?
5. Is citizen engagement or problem-solving part of your department's evaluation of you as an officer?
6. What systems are in place to prevent the adverse effects of a quota system, and how does the department ensure a focus on qualitative outcomes?

Citizens

1. How would you rate your local police department on a scale from 1-10?
2. In what ways can you, as a citizen, provide feedback on police performance and community safety concerns?
3. Does your local police department use a CompStat-like system to combat crime?
4. Does your local police department use any survey to gauge how good of a job it is doing?
5. What efforts is your local department making to avoid over-policing and ensure fair treatment for all community members?

CONCLUSION

Sir Robert Peel's principles, a testament to his vision, continue to echo through the annals of policing, resonating with the same vigor today as they did nearly two centuries ago. The principles advocate for community engagement, professionalism, and unwavering accountability, which are the cornerstones of modern law enforcement strategies that emphasize building public trust, thwarting crime, and affirming the supremacy of the law.

The timeless principles established by Sir Robert Peel serve as an enduring blueprint for effective and ethical policing. The underlying philosophy of these principles is to cultivate a harmonious relationship between law enforcement and the community, wherein the prevention of crime is paramount, the approval and cooperation of the public are sought after, and voluntary compliance with the law is preferred over coercive measures.

Peel's first principle advocates for proactive crime prevention, a strategy that is ever so pertinent in contemporary law enforcement. Modern policing endeavors, grounded in this principle, are diverse, encompassing community policing initiatives, intelligence-led policing models, and strategic crime prevention partnerships. These proactive approaches contribute to building safer communities by addressing the root causes of crime and employing preemptive strategies.

The second principle places significant weight on securing public approval, a facet that is increasingly vital in today's society, where the legitimacy of law enforcement is often challenged. Maintaining public trust is not merely an ideological goal but a practical necessity. Through endeavors that promote transparency, encourage open dialogue, and actively involve community members in safety initiatives, law enforcement agencies can strengthen their bond with the public, earning their approval and support.

The third principle emphasizes the importance of the public's willing cooperation with the police, a concept that resonates with the community-oriented policing models of today. The essence of this principle is the recognition that policing success is intrinsically linked to the community's trust and support. By establishing a foundation of mutual respect, safeguarding citizens' rights, and engaging them as active partners in crime prevention, police can secure the willing cooperation of the public, which is instrumental in maintaining social order and preventing crime.

Peel's fourth principle rightly asserts that the community's voluntary compliance with the law decreases when law enforcement resorts to using force. This understanding is critical, as it suggests that the power of the police stems from public approval of their existence, actions, and behavior rather than their ability to compel or coerce. Consequently, law enforcement needs to use force only when necessary and to ensure that when it is employed, it is proportional to the threat encountered. This careful use of force helps maintain the public's trust and willingness to cooperate.

The fifth principle revolves around the concept of impartiality in policing. The cornerstone of justice is the fair and unbiased application of the law without prejudice or preference for any individual or group. This principle is foundational in maintaining public confidence in the law enforcement system and ensuring all community members feel valued and protected.

The sixth principle addresses the necessity for restraint in using force, echoing a commitment to minimize harm and preserve life. This principle advocates for strategies prioritizing de-escalation and conflict resolution, reserving force as a last resort. Such an approach is ethical and instrumental in maintaining the sanctity of life and the dignity of individuals, which is paramount in a just society.

The seventh principle encapsulates the idea that the police are an extension of the public and vice versa. This perspective fosters a deep sense of community and shared responsibility for safety and order. It is the bedrock of community policing, a philosophy that encourages police officers to build strong, positive, and collaborative relationships with the communities they serve, ensuring that policing is responsive to the community's needs.

The eighth principle delineates the boundary between the functions of the police and the judiciary, ensuring that the role of law enforcement is distinct from that of adjudicating guilt or innocence. This separation is crucial for maintaining a fair and just legal system where due process is respected, and the rights of individuals are protected.

Lastly, the ninth principle posits that the presence of crime and disorder, not the visibility or actions of police, should measure a police force's success. This principle champions the belief that the true efficacy of policing is reflected in the absence of crime, achieved not through a show of force but through effective crime prevention and fostering a peaceful community.

The principles' enduring significance lies in their emphasis on community collaboration and ethical conduct. In an era marked by complex challenges, evolving technologies, and diverse populations, these principles provide a guiding light for law enforcement agencies seeking to navigate the intricacies of modern policing. The idea that *"the police are the public and the public are the police"* resonates more than ever, encouraging a shift towards community-oriented policing, fostering trust, and building solid partnerships.

Moreover, the principles' emphasis on minimum use of force, impartial service, and the importance of public cooperation serves as a counterbalance against potential abuses of power. By adhering to these principles, law enforcement agencies can ensure that their actions are rooted in fairness, justice, and the protection of civil liberties.

Furthermore, Peel's principles encourage a forward-looking approach to law enforcement by stressing crime prevention rather than mere reaction. The goal of achieving the absence of crime and disorder encourages innovative strategies, data-driven practices, and collaboration with social services to address the underlying causes of criminal behavior. This forward-thinking perspective aligns well with contemporary efforts to create safer and more resilient communities.

Integrating Sir Robert Peel's principles into contemporary policing involves recognizing society's constant evolution while upholding the timeless tenets of public service, fairness, and community partnership. In the digital age, where information flows freely, and communities are more diverse and interconnected, law enforcement must adapt these principles to address the nuanced demands of modern governance and social order.

Peel's vision, encapsulated in his nine principles, stresses the foundational role of ethical conduct, community trust, and the imperative to prevent crime proactively. As we step into the future, these principles guide law enforcement to engage with advanced technologies, data analytics, and community feedback mechanisms, all while ensuring that the essence of policing remains grounded in the public good.

In the 21st century, these principles are more than a historical footnote; they are the guiding ethos for a progressive, community-centric approach to policing. They advocate for a balance between traditional methods and innovative practices that respond to the dynamic nature of crime and societal expectations. Law enforcement agencies can embody these principles by leveraging technology for transparency, cultivating community relations through engagement programs, and constantly evaluating their strategies to ensure they align with the principles of justice.

By affirming Peel's enduring legacy in this way, law enforcement honors its past and charts a course for a future where police and the public work in concert for the safety and prosperity of all. This commitment to Peel's principles is a pledge to the kind of policing that respects the past, responds to the present, and is ready for future challenges.

ABOUT THE AUTHOR

Chief (Ret) Billy Grogan is a seasoned law enforcement veteran with over four decades of service, including a notable 15-year stint as the founding Chief of Police for the Dunwoody Police Department. Passionate about fostering robust, positive police-community relations, Chief Grogan is committed to empowering law enforcement leaders with the wealth of resources available at topcopleadership.com.

With a master's in public administration from Kennesaw State University and a distinguished alumnus of the FBI National Academy's 193rd Session, Chief Grogan's expertise is deep and broad. His voice resonates beyond the borders of the United States, reaching international law enforcement audiences in countries like Egypt, Hungary, and the Republic of Georgia.

A recognized authority on law enforcement's use of social media, Chief Grogan's written word and teachings have informed and helped shape modern policing strategies and practices. His presidency of the Georgia Association of Chiefs of Police and his long-standing role on the IACP Human and Civil Rights Committee reflect his dedication to leadership and civil liberties.

At the core of Chief Grogan's philosophy lies a staunch belief in fair and impartial policing, ensuring that citizens receive nothing less than the most honorable service.

ACKNOWLEDGMENTS

This book stands as a testament to the enduring patience and unwavering support of my wife, who has graciously navigated the ebb and flow of my writing journey over the past two years. Her profound tolerance for my endless musings and discussions about policing and community has been nothing short of heroic.

She has supported me throughout my law enforcement career and continues to do so regardless of the endeavor.

The seeds of this book were sown in the fertile ground of dialogue and interaction with my colleagues and readers. Your enthusiastic and thoughtful responses to my initial blog posts on my website have been the wind beneath the wings of this journey. Each comment and expression of interest watered the idea that these posts could grow into something more—into this book that now seeks to bridge the gap between law enforcement and the communities they serve across the nation.

RESOURCES

If you have enjoyed learning more about Sir Robert Peel's 9 Principles of Policing and would like to display a high-quality poster of them at home or work, check out the following posters:

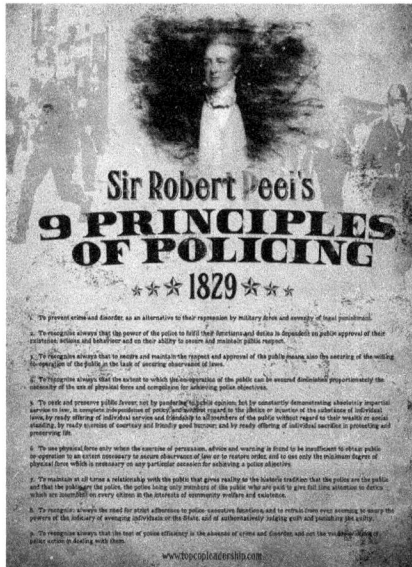

https://billyjgrogan.com/peelretroposter

https://billyjgrogan.com/peelmodernposter

Also, consider embracing the essence of valor and dedication with this inspiring poster, "Guardians of the Community."

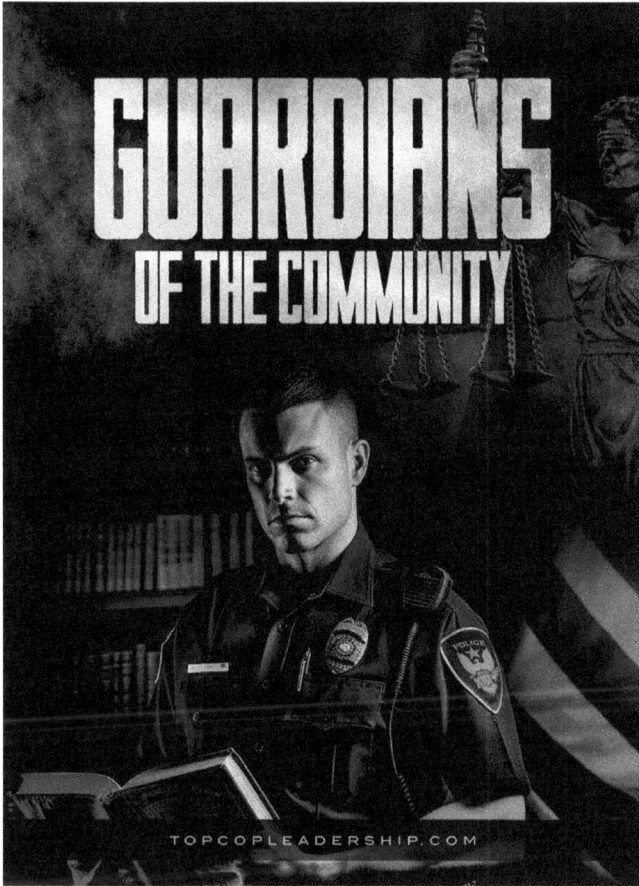

https://billyjgrogan.com/guardiansposter

www.ingramcontent.com/pod-product-compliance
Lightning Source LLC
Chambersburg PA
CBHW060226030426
42335CB00014B/1348